CLOUDS
OVER
FEDERALISM
The Real Working of the Indian Polity

CLOUDS OVER FEDERALISM

The Real Working of the Indian Polity

AKHTAR MAJEED

MANAK
PUBLICATIONS PVT. LTD

First Edition 2010

Published by

MANAK

PUBLICATIONS PVT. LTD

B-7, Saraswati Complex, Subhash Chowk,
Laxmi Nagar, New Delhi 110092
Phone: 22453894, 22042529
E-mail : manak_publications@hotmail.com
manak.publications@gmail.com

USA Office

8145 KOLB AVE, ALLEN PARK, M.I. 48101 USA
E-mail: rahul_upma@yahoo.com

ISBN 978-81-7831-215-6

Layout by
KHUSHNUMA

Laser Typeset by
T. ALI
Hamdard Nagar, New Delhi

Printed in India by
Nice Printing Press, New Delhi

Contents

1

Introduction

Federal systems require inter-governmental processes and institutions for tackling the unavoidable questions concerning overlapping jurisdictions. There are many variations among these federations in their institutional design, the character of the diversity within their societies, their degree of economic development, and their policy agendas. Nevertheless a common feature among them has been the need for effective internal inter-governmental arrangements. Thus, while there is no single federal model or example that is applicable everywhere, there is much to be gained from examining the similarities and differences in their approaches to facilitating federal-provincial and inter-provincial cooperation and co-ordination. Since many of the problems are common to virtually all federations, examining the experience of other federations in institutionalising intergovernmental relations may provide us with both positive and negative lessons, i.e. with both effective examples and cautionary tales.

The essence of federalism is the existence of independent political decision-making at different levels of government. Yet, such decision-making cannot operate in isolation and inter-dependence in governance necessitates shared-governance. The philosophical foundation of the US federalism stipulated that a government is best if it governs the least and, therefore, only limited functions were given to the Union. This option did not exist in India because already there was a long historical tradition of centralisation of power and authority. Our philosophical foundation was that a government is best when it is able to bring about social transformation. Hence, the framers of the Constitution and the subsequent law-makers consciously ensured that the overwhelming majority of powers and authority was kept with the Union. In the process, we overlooked a philosophical foundation of our independence struggle: good governance is no substitute for self-governance. We discarded the federal principle that even if a function is not done best by a regional government, that power should not be assumed by the Union. This was not only against an accepted federal norm but also against the democratic principle of self-rule. The sharing of powers between Union and states came to a situation in which the Union had what powers it had but shared in the powers that the states had.

The spirit of the Constitution was not on exclusiveness but on shared coordination. What has evolved is as if Union's powers are exclusive powers and States' powers are shared powers. This is creating serious problems for working of a federal system and it need to be studied and taken care of. The Constitution of India is a mechanism for sharing power in our social-pluralism that is territorially identified. The Constitution had envisaged a 'creative balance' between the need for an effective Union/ Centre and effectively – empowered states. The federal system that emerged became the sound framework for the working of our Constitution. In spite of problems of balance-maintenance, the system has survived, though many of its federal features got eroded. In spite of great odds and great complexity, India as a nation has survived, because it is united as a Nation with the voluntary and natural agreement of its constituent units. Largely, this is due to the fact that the Constitution has worked as a functioning mechanism not just for resolving inter-governmental disputes but in maintaining a constitutional balance between the tiers of government.

The question of distribution of responsibilities and assignment of resources is linked to political culture also. It is not as if it is only now that we have started thinking whether this distribution is generally compatible with our society, political culture and economy. These concerns were before the makers of the Constitution also. It was definitely a concern that India, with so many of regional diversities, needed a centralised planning. It was a concern that some planned development was needed to remove regional disparities. Maintenance of unity and national integration was a major concern. The question is whether federalism was more compatible with the Indian society of 1947 or is it more relevant for our society at the beginning of the 21st Century. There is a widely-held scholarly belief that our society has largely remained stagnant. One perceptible change that has emerged is the emergence of the erstwhile non-participant actors, such as Dalits, the Backwards and some marginalised sections of minorities. The federalisation of the party system has altered the basic premises of inter-governmental relations, and has created new mechanisms that are impacting on the federal structure. It has led to the development of new ways of organising inter-states and the Union-states relations. Most of these newly-evolved structures are informal, even ad hoc, even 'para-constitutional.' All this has affected not only party politics and legislative configuration, but also the nature of political coalitions and alliances, inter-governmental relations and, consequently, the nature of distribution of responsibilities among governments at different levels.

Any discussion about distribution of powers and responsibilities would encompass the constitutional mechanisms that have been used for that end. It appears as if the constitutional discourse is about 'selection' of powers and not about the 'description' of powers that are to be distributed. Thus, existing provisions regarding our federal structure need to be particularly examined from the evolving perspectives of autonomy (of states, regions, institutions) and integration (*i.e.*, unity and diversity). We have to balance the factors promoting federal-institutional model of self-rule with shared rule. The inherent notion of power-distribution and power-sharing arrangements is a question between the National and Regional constituents of our federation. This relationship between the sub-structures of Union and states is to be examined from the notion of competence – division and sharing of a subject. Areas of potential federal conflicts, that invite attention, include working of several constitutional provisions about Union's intervention in spheres of States' activities, distribution of financial resources, and other issues of fiscal federalism. It would not be sufficient, or appropriate, to assert that there is too much of centralisation because it is not the same level of centralisation or decentralisation in all subjects.

There are structural changes that have been introduced in the Indian federal system. This is an emergence of a sub-states structure and an evolution of multi-level federalism. This third tier is not functioning in isolation but is interacting with a range and variety of non-government institutions and voluntary-sector institutions. This interface has had an effect not only on a third tier but also on the other two, in a federal system. Any debate on a distribution of responsibility and of resources would remain incomplete if a constitutional position of the federal structure remains blurred, even after half a century of constitution working. Are the local bodies—the third tier—'institutions of self-government' (Article 243 G) or are they 'units of self-government' (Article 40)? Under which term are they merely an implementing agency of the Union and states projects, and under which terms do they acquire some autonomous status to discharge their responsibilities with commensurate resources to do the same? When funds are not allotted, and funds and functionaries are not given, and any independent status is merely on paper, then any conceptual, theoretical or action- analysis of the working of such 'tiers of government' is not possible. This is possible only after certain status-ambiguities are first resolved. Are they instruments of popular democracy for empowerment of the citizens or are they an instrument for better implementation of governance? Is this so-called 'third-tier' an institution of empowerment or an institution of governance? Because of the nature of Indian society, the type of problems that we face, the diversities that exist, and the possibilities of making decisions at that level, it is high time that it is regarded as a third level of government and not just some unit to provide civic amenities.

Even if there is some substance in what has been constitutionally provided to the local-level governments, much of it has been eroded due to compulsions of power-play. Nobody, who has power, wants to surrender it voluntarily and nobody is willing to empower another at own cost. The growth of local-level leadership is perceived as a threat by the entrenched national and states elite. Yet, we talk of local-level governments as instruments of empowerment and governance. In this talk of empowerment, what is overlooked is our own competence to empower 'the lower, the third tier.' It is a condescending approach which assumes that power rightfully belongs only to the Union and the states and they, in their abundant wisdom, have devolved power on the 'third tier,' empowering the local-level governments. The system can work if we accept that power belongs to the people who give it to the next tier upward, and then next tier further upward. In the so-called empowerment of the local-level governments, actually the power gets transferred from one set of elite to another. In the Indian rural power-structure, so much of inequality exists that this empowerment may actually strengthen inequality and oppression.

One of upcoming issues with which Indian federalism would have to deal with is the changing nature of law and order issues and of terrorism. Dealing with new types of law and order situation is no longer possible for any one states. It has become a national issue but there are clear differences between political parties over this. Union's position, while dealing with different states over this issue, is also not above board. For political considerations, the Union remains inactive when some states do not implement this Act and, for different poll considerations, the Union protests its implementation by other states. Cyber crimes, and other types of white-collar crimes, are not limited to boundaries of a states and are national and international issues. There is a federal dimension in dealing with issues that transcend states boundaries: under whose powers is issue of law and order? If the Union intervenes in states boundaries for tackling law and order problems, it would become a contentious issue.

The liberalisation of national economy, and deregulation of the latter, have transformed the states from being a regulator to a facilitator. No doubt, even a federal states would have to regulate, but a facilitating states would regulate differently. It is in this context that the issue of a supposed-paradigm shift needs to be analyzed. Is it because of a deregulation and economic opening up that the Chief Ministers of states are in a position to directly negotiate foreign investment for their states? Or, because of their political clout and the considerations of political coalitions, the Union government allows some of them to so impact on our federal structure and inter-government relations. It is not just a globalised economy that the States' Chief Ministers are in a position to deal directly with other countries. It is due to compulsions of coalition politics and political alliances that the Union conveniently looks the other way. Set conventions are yet to evolve but states governments are establishing their own offices in other countries to attract foreign investment. Is this constitutionally permissible? Were they not part of a ruling coalition, the Union might have taken this as a diversion from constitution and institutional framework of federalism.

There is another problem that comes out of the ongoing 'globalisation' of decisions, policies, services and economics. In the light of the fast-emerging global governance, there may not be any power left to share between different governments within a country. For instance, environmental law and its framing have ceased to be matters of our concern. We are signatories of certain international Protocols and conventions and we have no option but to implement laws so framed by certain international institutions. Since our options are so limited, it does not matter who shares what or who works. If there is no power left to share, we cannot conceive of sharing powers at a union, states and local levels. Once the states as such becomes depoliticised and, subsequently, redundant, then even if powers are decentralised it won't matter.

Federalism does not devote relationships only between a Union and a states, but not much attention has been given to need for cooperation between states. There are no constitutional rules governing a relationship between two states, and it is the Union which dictates these relations. There are various issues of conflicts between states, such as river-water distribution, where inter-states cooperation is required just as it is needed for tackling problems of law and order cutting across states boundaries. There is another dimension and equally relevant too. Regional disparities have increased during the last 50 years. It seems that, instead of any lack of decentralisation, it is decentralisation that has made it easier for the states not to discharge responsibilities entrusted to them. They have been given so much to implement that they do not implement at all. Shirking their own responsibilities, states look towards the Union. This aspect of Indian federalism is still not clear. Is it a questions of constitutional framework of distribution of powers and responsibilities? Is it due to a lack of funding provided to the states by the Union? Or, whether states have not exercised their responsibilities that they were supposed to do?

In most of the contemporary states and societies, certain federal practices can be instruments not just of good governance but also of conflict management. They include power-sharing, people's participation, devolution of power and authority, and inter-governmental collaboration. This is particularly so in plural societies—that form an overwhelming majority in the international community. In such societies, issues of unity with diversity, self-rule and peaceful resolution of contentious issues, between tiers of government, have attracted attention and growing interest of scholars and practitioners of federalism.

The need for intergovernmental collaborative institutions and processes, has led to an emphasis upon 'cooperative federalism' within most federations, although the extent of this has varied greatly from those where duality and exclusivity of powers have been strongly emphasized to those where shared and concurrent jurisdiction have received greater emphasis.

What is presented in the following pages is the Indian experience of working of a federal polity. The structure and working of inter-government relations in India have been discussed innumerable times, in detail, in many useful studies. Not only do we know, by now, what is wrong with the system and its working, we also know why it is not seriously been corrected. What the present study does is to re-interpret formulations in the light of contextual changes. As a theory of development, Federalism concerns itself with competence and autonomy, and it is in this context that issue of its working is discussed. The emerging social realities are affecting political situation and, in these pages, an attempt has been made to study how political situation and public policy are affecting our federal structure.

1 January 2010 *Akhtar Majeed*

2

India: A Federal Nation

The insensitive treatment, by the Indian ruling elite, of popular demands, has often forced people to confine themselves within the ethnic/ group boundaries, mostly within the confines of minority groups, consolidating these bonds, and making way for more powerful assertions of their identities. When ethnic groups feel that nationalism is inadequate in providing emotional satisfaction of security they turn towards more familiar bonds of caste/sub-nationalism or linguistic- religious identities. These identities are considered more responsive to individual or group aspirations. When such groups become conscious of their identities and ask for a bigger piece of cake then power-sharing through Federalism becomes the easy and effective solution.

In a plural nation, both the majority and the minority(ies) need the "other" to build-up and consolidate their own identity and interests. "Pampering of the minority" and the "discrimination by the majority" serve this purpose. It is by distinguishing 'us' from 'them' that social groups promote their perceptions of superiority over others. Tolerance of minorities is not the response of the modern part of a majority. It is the traditional way of life that has, over the centuries, developed tolerance over the others. It was the traditional majority of India that tolerated Christianity here before it reached Europe and that tolerated Islam from before the time it became a politically dominant force here. It is the modernised majority, uprooted from traditional values, uncertain about its own identity, desperate in forging a distinct identity yet indirectly forging one similar to those whom it is opposing—a majority with a minority complex—which is intolerant towards the minorities.

Often, the term 'minorities' is described in India as those groups which are outside the majority (that is, Hindu). It implies that the core of Indian identity is Hinduism. It also implies that minorities are outside this mainstream (and, hence, outside the Indian nation) until they 'Indianise.' But it also implies that only religious groups, that are numerically smaller, can be minorities. In fact, regional, ethnic, tribal, caste groups can also perceive themselves suffering from discrimination, being subordinate to the others; and in this way their minority status is self-defined. It is their method of attracting attention to their perceived deprivation and to their position of being disadvantaged.

Any monolithic definition of nationalism, in a plural society, is bound to create a situation of conflict between the majority and the minorities. A greater community-mobilization or community-consciousness should not be a matter of alarm in a plural society, unless the goal is an assimilation of ethnic groups. Greater community-consciousness can be 'communitarianism' but it need not be communal. Even articulation of revivalism or a going back to only the basic principles of one's religion ['fundamentalism'] cannot be communal. It is when communitarianism looks at the 'other' with suspicion and hatred that it becomes communal. It is when this 'other,' they, are identified as the cause of the decline in the fortunes of 'our' community that the basis of communalism is established. It is when irreconcilable political interests dominate inter-community relationship that communalism is constructed. Otherwise, as in the Constitution of India, the community loyalties should be viewed as various levels of a wider national loyalty, crystallizing themselves at different gradients with different sectional interests, which in their totality are the best interests of national integration. It is when attempts are made to crush these loyalties that national integration is jeopardized.

In India, the Constitution recognizes the nature of ethnic identity and makes adequate arrangements for its accommodation. The Constitution has not ignored the differences based on religion, language etc. It does not discourage them but only says that no one is to be put to any disability based on such differences. In fact, instead of discouraging these differences, the Constitution takes them for granted and offers every facility for their expression and development, i.e., Articles 19(1), 25, 26, 27, 28, 29 & 30. Whereas Articles 14, 15, 16 & 19 deny inequality, Articles 25 to 30 confer privileges; and there is no contradiction involved. The Constitution recognizes ethnic-plurality of the Indian society and gives scope for their expression, both to the individual (Art. 19) and to groups of them (Art. 25, 26, 29 & 30). The result of all this, put together, is that every citizen can exercise his privileges in the name of religion and culture, and nobody can do that in the name of religion and culture what he cannot do as a citizen. In this context, the implications of Article 30 of the Constitution may be taken as an example. This Article confers on linguistic and religious minorities the right to establish and administer educational institutions of their choice. Actually, this is a fundamental right that should have been given to all the citizens, but exigencies of a multi-ethnic society conferred this right especially on religious - linguistic minorities. They are given a right to transmit their culture through their educational institutions. It is recognised that the language and culture etc of a minority community can be preserved through educational institutions and, therefore, the right to establish and maintain educational institutions of its own is conferred upon a minority, by the Constitution. Interestingly, in a Supreme Court judgement [*Jagdev Singh v. Pratap Singh, A 1965 SC 183*], it was held that the right to conserve language includes the right to agitate for the protection of that language, including political agitation. Even if our society were not plural, not multi-ethnic, with one religion and one language, we still would have needed some guarantee against states monopoly of education. The right under this Article is not merely a minority right but a fundamental democratic right, based on the freedom to dissent from the majority view. Without this freedom, integration would only be assimilation. As in respect to many of our other rights, the Courts in India have ever been vigilant in checking the governmental actions that tend to erode educational rights of the minorities.

When different social groups try to maintain distinctive attributes and identities, in the real pursuit of some material benefits, usually the result is a manifestation of various caste, religious, language, tribal and cultural assertions. Such assertions are usually the manifestation of demands for the creation of separate units in a federal set-up. Regionalism becomes the response of regional / linguistic minority groups against unequal sharing of the benefits of developmental activity, and a protest against the stabilisation and monopolisation of advantages through policies aiming at the institutionalisation of existing stratification system, which is the result of cumulative de-equalisation and power-inequality. There is no attempt to check the gravitation of power in the hands of the national elite and no check on the proliferation of asymmetrical development. The response of the constituting units, in a plural-federal society, is the manifestation of greater regionalism. Such demands by regional minorities have not gone beyond claiming resource-sharing within the broader national context. In such a situation, cultural and ethnic differences form the basis of separatist movements. Such demands may be accompanied by or may be a sequel to preferential treatment Cultural differences, in themselves, may not be the causes of regional and nativist movements but they certainly are present in such conflicts; and magnifying of such differences is the political technique to define cultural and political identity. The demands for autonomy and special status are not just protests of regional nature but are also assertions for cultural and economic rights. The protest is against the economic exploitation of a particular territory by culturally different people. The apprehension is regarding the outside-exploitation of 'our' resources and marginalisation of 'our' identity. When different social groups try to maintain distinctive attributes and identities, in the real pursuit of some material benefits, usually the result is a manifestation of various caste, religious, language, tribal and cultural assertions. Such assertions are usually the manifestation of demands for the creation of separate units in a federal set-up. In India, regionalism has been the response of regional/linguistic minority groups against unequal sharing of the benefits of developmental activity, has been a protest against the stabilisation and monopolisation of advantages through policies aiming at the institutionalisation of existing stratification system, has been the result of cumulative de-equalisation and power-inequality.

A misconception is the belief that an ethnic, religious group would become modernised only when it's distinct religious solidarity and identity is superseded and, in this task, the Personal Law appears the biggest barrier in the supposed modernisation of a minority community. In fact, the idea of a uniform civil code, in place of a distinct personal law for a particular religious group, cannot have precedence over the right of a community to it's own cultural identity. It is more important that the code should be just and fair and enlightened than that it should be uniform. Right of cultural identity is the 'Natural Right' carrying which an ethnic group becomes a part of the social whole. Personal law is the manifestation of this Natural Right. Minorities, particularly, treat their Personal Law as a symbol of their ethnic-cultural identity and the fact of their being in a minority helps in strengthening their belief. It makes them hold on rigidly to all their distinctive possessions in an attempt to preserve their identity, particularly since the demand to change such identity comes from outside the group.

Different types of minorities, in different regions, have been made to live under guilt of being poor and backward and under-developed and, therefore, a drag on the national development. The general desperations and deprivations of the social life, and the consequent frustrations and anger of the society, are tactically directed and channelised against the minority groups, presenting them as the villain for many of the above frustrations. A conscious effort is made to paint a viscous image of the minorities, through mass media, and by the distortion of historical – social facts. 'They' are now blamed for all the evils in the Indian society. As the country limps from one crisis to another, the fascists point out towards the "pampered and appeased" minorities as the cause of each crisis. Even the most congenial among the majority have been seduced to believe that the minorities have been appeased too long, too much. The number is not small that wants to keep the Muslims and the Sikhs on a permanent probation regarding their patriotism and loyalty to the nation. The idea is to develop further guilt among them. The guilt, along with the occasional 'riots' are intended to develop a fear psychosis among them, leading to a deep sense of inferiority complex. The objective is clearly a total control and political domination over them.

The dichotomy is that while the political assertiveness of the erstwhile disadvantaged social groups is seen as a sign of robust and dynamic Indian democracy, similar political moves by the religious minorities are considered as 'fundamentalism,' communalism and worse. Ultimately, it is not just the question of majority-minority in a plural society; it is the question of social and distributive justice in a liberal democracy. If democracy is not receptive to various identities in a plural society then it remains only a majoritarian democracy that 'disprivileges' the minorities, a steam-rolling system in which it is valid to override the minorities if, numerically, they are insignificant and, politically and economically, powerless. The viable alternative is that which has been provided under the Constitution of India. Since the democratic procedures and institutions, in the normal course, would work in a manner that would be disadvantageous to the minorities, the states has to ensure special provisions for the protection of minority rights.

For the national development of a country like India, social justice, economic progress and political democracy have to be based on national integration, and for the achievement of that end the technique adopted was secularism. The normally accepted meaning of the term 'secularism' does not signify the neutrality of the Indian states in religious matters and equal opportunity for all religions to grow, subject as according to Article 25 of the Constitution, 'to public order, morality and health.'

This tolerance comes out of the acceptance of our cultural heritage as 'many-splendoured thing.' The Indian commitment to secularism is not a concession to the minorities by the majority, nor is it an obligation of the circumstances that India is a pluralist society. The compulsions of a free society would have obliged us to be a secular society even if no pluralism were involved and there were no religious minorities. Secularism is not an obligation placed on us but an evidence of our commitment to the establishment of a modern and free society. In the political sense, secularism is the refutation of the totalitarian concept of the states. It takes away from the state's sphere of concern certain areas of individual interest and endeavour where the states has no role to play. This does not mean that it places some limitation on the states-sovereignty. On the other hand, it emphasises that a free and open states is so sovereign that it does not have to live in fear of ideas and faiths, nor does it fear that it could be subverted by such beliefs. This positive quality of fearlessness is more to be cherished and respected than the negative sense of a grudging tolerance that secularism is sometimes picturised as. The whole point of secularism is its courageous hospitality to ideas where dissident views are not treated as an affront to majority opinion. This is the idea behind Indian secularism: Not just a passive tolerance but an active encouragement to religious pluralism. To make a distinction with the traditional Western concept of secularism, the Indian connotation is not anti-religious or irreligious and, therefore, the Indian states tacitly gives official support to different forms of religiosity. This 'religion-dominated' secularism has led to the maintenance of the traditional religious orientation as a feature of the Indian society and to the strengthening of pride in religious identities. And this is a 'basic structure' of the Indian society that gets reflected in the Indian Constitution.

There is no reason, and there should be no reason, for any citizen in public life to be secret and apologetic about his beliefs. There is no contradiction in being a staunch believer in some faith and in being secularist because Indian secularism does not mean 'irreligion.' Besides, Indian secularism has hitched ethnicity to politics in a more or less pragmatic way. Indeed, the new political institutions in India have acquired popular support and cultural content from precisely the same new entrants from what was till now an ethnic hinterland. With their entries, the public life in India has got an identifiable 'Indian style." With this tremendous political mobilisation and participation, it is not possible to disinfect those entering the public life from religion and ethnicity. Naturally, the other course open is for the states to follow a policy of non-alignment in its relations with different religions within it.

Often, the term 'minorities' is described in India as those groups which are outside the majority (that is, Hindu). It implies that the core of Indian identity is Hinduism. It also implies that minorities are outside this mainstream (and, hence, outside the Indian nation) until they 'Indianise.' But it also implies that only religious groups, that are numerically smaller, can be minorities. In fact, regional, ethnic, tribal, caste groups can also perceive themselves suffering from discrimination, being subordinate to the others; and in this way their minority status is self-defined. It is their method of attracting attention to their perceived deprivation and to their position of being disadvantaged.

Feelings of sub-nationalism have developed against such minority groups when the natives in a region have failed to effectively compete against the minority coming from outside (e.g., anti-Bihari feelings in Maharashtra and Assam) in matters of employment, trade and commerce and when these 'others' were culturally distinct and visible and could easily be blamed for 'our' failures. Protectionist demands among the majority groups in a region have manifested, in many regions in India, out of an aggressive nationalism and antagonistic regionalism, from people who feel they are the deprived ones. Such a perception might have been based on false consiousness and false aspirations but it grasped the sub-conciousness of people in Assam, Telengana, Maharashtra, Marathawad, Uttarakhand, Punjab and Kashmir. That sub-consciousness had provided them with an opportunity to symbolically overcome their apprehensions, their inabilities, their failures.

Unfortunately, secularism has been reduced to mere rhetoric, a slogan, an scoring-board for dubious electoral advantages. Secularism is not a goal of democracy and social justice but only a method of achieving the same, a means of maintaining social harmony by removing religion as a devisive factor in politics. Secularism is only a method of good governance in a plural society. And good governance is not 'appeasement,' either of the minority or of the majority. It is a right of "We, the People of India." It is by distinguishing 'us' from 'them' that social groups promote their perceptions of superiority over others. Tolerance of minorities is not the response of the modern part of a majority. It is the traditional way of life that has, over the centuries, developed tolerance over the others. It was the traditional majority of India that tolerated Christianity here before it reached Europe and that tolerated Islam from before the time it became a politically dominant force here. It is the modernised majority, uprooted from traditional values, uncertain about its own identity, desperate in forging a distinct identity yet indirectly forging one similar to those whom it is opposing—a majority with a minority complex—which is intolerant towards the minorities.

The very concept of a 'national culture' is often questioned, particularly by the minorities in a plural society, in view of traditional divisions between high and low cultures. Can the 'culture of the majority' be termed as the national culture or the latter has to include variants and colours of all the streams in the nation? What is usually overlooked is that the political interests govern and regulate the cultural interests and, in the process, define a particular version of culture. Otherwise, in fact, culture does not segment society but plucks unity from diversity. There can be no option for a plural society between 'unity' or 'diversity' because both have to co-exist in a single framework. That has been the beauty of the Indian federal nation.

Further Readings

Ahmad, Aijaz, *Lineages of the Present-Political Essays*, (New Delhi: Tulika, 1996).

Arora, Balveer and Douglas Verney, *Multiple Identities in a Single states: Indian Federalism in a Comparative Perspective*, (New Delhi: Konark, 1999).

Baird, Robert (ed.), *Religion in Modern India*, (New Delhi: Manohar, 1995).

Bakshi, P.M., *The Constitution of India*, (Delhi: Universal Law Pub., 2003).

Basu, Kaushik and Sanjay Subrahmaniam, *Unravelling the Nation: Sectarian Conflict and India's Secular Identity*, (New Delhi: Penguin, 1996).

Bhargava, Rajeev (ed.), *Secularism and its Critics,* (Delhi: Oxford University Press, 1998).

Brass, Paul R. and Achin Vanaik, *Competing Nationalisms in India,* (New Delhi: Orient Longmans, 2001).

Chandhoke, Neera, *The Conceits of Civil Society,* (New Delhi: Oxford, 2003).

Chaubey, P.K., *Fiscal Federalism in India,* (Deep & Deep: New Delhi 2003) Chadda, Maya, *Ethnicity, Security and Separatism in India,* (New York: Columbia University Press, 1997). N. Chandhoke, *Beyond Secularism: The Rights of Religious Minorities,* (Delhi: Oxford University Press, 1999).

Crossman, Brenda and Ratna Kapur, *Secularism's Last Sigh,* (New Delhi: Oxford University Press, 2001).

Dua, B.D. and M.P. Singh (ed.), *Indian Federalism in the New Millennium,* (New Delhi: Manohar, 2003).

Gupta, Dipankar, *Culture, Space and the Nation-States,* (New Delhi: Sage, 2000).

Gurr, Ted Robert, *Minorities at Risk: A Global View of Ethnopolitical Conflict,* (Washington, 1993).

Hansen, T.B., *The Saffron Wave: Democracy and Hindu Nationalism in Modern India,* (Princeton: Princeton University Press, 1999).

Hansen, T.B., *Violence in Urban India: Identity Politics, Mumbai and the Postcolonial City,* (Delhi: Permanent Black, 2002)

Jayal, Niraja Gopal, *Democracy and the states: Welfare, Secularism and Development in Contemporary India,* (Delhi: Oxford University Press, 1999).

Jenkins, Rob (ed.), *Regional Reflections: Comparing Politics Across India's states,* (New Delhi: Oxford, 2004).

Jodhka, Surinder S., *Community and Identity: Contemporary Discourse On Culture and Politics In India,* (New Delhi: Sage, 2001).

Kaviraj, Sudipta and Sunil Khilnani, *Civil Society—History and Possibilities,* (Cambridge: Cambridge University Press, 2001).

Kohli, Atul and Amrita Basu, *Community Conflicts and the States in India,* (Delhi: Oxford University Press, 1998).

Kymlicka, Will, *Multicultural Citizenship: A Liberal Theory of Minority Rights,* (Oxford: Clarendon Press, 1995).

Mahajan, Gurpreet (ed.), *The Multicultural Path: Issues of Diversity and Discrimination in Democracy*, (New Delhi, 2002).

Majeed, Akhtar, *Federal India: Design for Good Governance*, (New Delhi: Manak, 2005).

Majeed, Akhtar, *Federalism Within the Union*, (New Delhi: Manak, 2004).

Oommen, T.K., *Nation, Civil Society and Social Movements*, (New Delhi: Konark, 2001

Oommen, T.K. (ed.), *Citizenship and National Identity-from Colonialism to Globalism*, (New Delhi: Sage, 1997).

Oommen, T.K., *State and Society in India: Studies in Nation-Building*, (New Delhi: Sage, 1990).

Pylee, M.V., *Our Constitution, Government and Politics*, (New Delhi: Universal Law, 2002).

Roy, Ramashray, *The Federal Experience: India and Russia*, (New Delhi: Shipra, 2003).

Vanaik, Achin, *Communalism Contested: Religion, Modernity and Secularization*, (Delhi: Vistaar, 1997).

Varshney, Ashutosh, *Ethnic Conflict and Civic Life*, (New Delhi: Oxford, 2002).

3

The Changing Politics of States' Reorganization

There has been a welcome change in attitude, among the Indian ruling elite, in no longer treating states' reorganization as the emergence of parochial identities. Different regions established their identity on the basis of language, culture, administrative coherence, economic development, or lack of it. Gradually, it has been recognized that the reorganization of states leads to good governance if such reorganization stems from administrative convenience, economic viability, similarity in developmental needs of a subregion, and cultural-linguistic affinity.

India is not only large but also incredibly diverse. In religion, while it is predominantly Hindu, there are sizeable numbers of Sikhs, Jains, Buddhists, Christians, and Muslims scattered throughout the land. In language, Hindi is predominant but is spoken by only nearly one-half of the population. There are nearly a score of official languages. Yet this broad brush does not convey the diversity present in most of India's states, regions, and localities.

After independence, the Union government's main

concern was to avoid anything like the partition that led to the creation of East and West Pakistan. There was no question that India had to be a federation, if only for administrative convenience. However, the hope of Jawaharlal Nehru and his colleagues was that the various states would be large and heterogeneous. Such "composite" states would discourage the emergence of parochial identities. However, it was not to be. As early as 1956, because of popular pressure, the 27 states were reorganized as 14 states that took account of the country's linguistic diversity. States' reorganization has continued. India is in constant flux as it creates new states in response to new demands for autonomy.

Many countries have had difficulty in maintaining their national identity in the face of demands for autonomy and even secession. The United Kingdom has still not resolved what used to be called "the Irish Question." Canada remains unsure about the future of Quebec. Former federations such as the USSR and Yugoslavia collapsed. Nigeria's federation is under siege. Western Europeans are moving toward a loose form of confederation, but are worried about the integration of Eastern Europe, and still more about Muslim Turkey as a potential EU member.

How, then, has heterogeneous India managed to remain intact? One explanation lies in what Indians call "states' reorganization." This involves both the adjustment of states boundaries and the creation of new states, both of which are the prerogative of the Union government ("the Center"). In the last decade, as India has become less centralized, the politics of states' reorganization have changed.

During the first half a century of independence, there were two opposing views. One, held by the Center, was that states should be economically viable and administratively convenient. The other, held by emerging groups, was that where there is a sense of community, or consciousness of a separate identity, then, if feasible, that community should form a separate states. The two views clashed, but over time, and often after violent confrontations, the second view prevailed, and once the centralized Congress party lost power, to be replaced by coalitions containing representatives of the states, the traditional hostility of the Government of India to states' reorganization weakened.

The Reluctance to Recognize the federal Reality

In 2009, there were 29 states in the Indian Union, together with seven union territories. In 1951, there had been 27 states, but the States' Reorganization Act of 1956 reduced these to 14. The number of states slowly increased, the the last one created in the latter part of 2009 and before that in 2000. But whereas previous demands for statehood had met with hostility from the Government of India, these states were created without the usual fuss.

Throughout the world, there have been numerous arguments in favor of the formation or reorganization of states. Among them are geographical proximity, a common language, similar usages and customs, comparable socioeconomic and political stages of development, common historical traditions and experiences, a common way of living, administrative expediency, and, more than anything else, a widely prevalent sentiment of "togetherness," that is, a sense of shared identity. Until recently, the Government of India did not favor arguments based on a common identity. Its preference was for administrative expediency. It was willing to establish large (50-100 million people) heterogeneous (or "composite") states with no particular sense of identity, the aim being administrative decentralization, nor were those groups concerned with development any more receptive to arguments stressing identity. The demand that a region become a states was until recently treated as a threat to national integration and coherence. A positive role was rarely acknowledged for these demands, even though they generated political participation. At one time or another, all the national political parties opposed the formation of new states. Whenever the demands were conceded, considerable struggle and much violence accompanied the process. There were charges of exploitation and counter-charges that the motives of those making the demands were parochial, fissiparous, and even anti-national. There was much resistance from the Union government.

Even changes to states borders (one form of states' reorganization) to accommodate people of the same language were granted very reluctantly. As early as 1947, the first prime minister, Jawaharlal Nehru, opposed the formation of states based on linguistic lines. He thought it would lead to the development of sub-nationalities that would ultimately agitate to become sovereign states.[1] This reluctance to accept the linguistic basis of regionalism, for fear of generating radical mass upsurges, was understandable. After all, in the 1920s, mass mobilization was precisely the purpose for which the nationalist elite had proposed reorganization of the provinces, as a tactic against foreign rule. Equating nationalism with the status quo was therefore nothing new.

The half-hearted reorganization of states in 1956 created the impression of a reluctant Center bowing to the pressures of "fissiparous tendencies" in the regions of various states. The reorganization was "half-hearted" in the sense that it was almost forced upon a reluctant Center, and the reorganization was also not complete because all the linguistic areas were not given territorial recognition. These regions were often not treated as politically coherent units reflecting the aspirations of their inhabitants to manage their own affairs. In this competition for resources, the regions used several benchmarks to establish their identity. They were language, culture, economic advancement, administrative coherence, and even the socioeconomic backwardness of the region (due to its being part of a bigger regional unit). Regional movements sparked demands for the formation of new states, and for the reorganization of existing states. These demands did not usually go beyond claiming resource sharing within the broader national context. In this, language was often the symbol giving expression to these aspirations.

The Rationale of the Demand for Reorganisation

With some 30 demands for new states being made currently, it may be time to rethink India's federal structure. The traditional view of the Center that the creation of new states encourages parochial and anti-national tendencies has been reconsidered because reorganization may serve good governance if four requirements are met: (1) administrative convenience, (2) economic viability, (3) similarity in the developmental needs of a sub- region, and (4) cultural-linguistic affinity. Therefore, the view of the Center that the creation of new states encourages parochial and anti-national tendencies needs to be modified, if not discarded. The argument is not for the subdivision of larger states, even for administrative convenience. However, a demand for reorganization need not necessarily threaten the unity of the country. At the same time, it should be remembered that historically, states' reorganization has occurred for various reasons. These have not necessarily met the Center's preference for "rational reorganization," nor have they always advanced good governance.

Whether the demand for a new states succeeds depends on much more than rationality. The people must have become emotionally involved in the process. They must have developed a distinct socio-cultural geographical identity. There must be the perception of systemic neglect of the region (i.e., a sense of"internal colonialism"). There has to be a popular movement in favor of a new states. Finally, there have to be leaders able to ignite and sustain such a movement.

A number of states (among them Assam, West Bengal, Andhra Pradesh, Maharashtra, and Uttar Pradesh) have witnessed demands for separate states from identifiable regions. Such regionalism has often emerged as a consequence of "mal-development" and the fear of some that they are being left out. When some ethnic groups move ahead more rapidly than others, parts of a region or states may not develop, leading to a distinguishable undeveloped region. Such a region may cover a small area within a states, and may, for economic-geographical, linguistic, and social reasons, possess a distinct identity. During the linguistic-regional agitations in Andhra Pradesh and Maharashtra, for example, the claims and significance of regional problems resulted from historical and economic factors. These encouraged the growth of political subcultures in unity of language, culture, and caste that were ultimately represented by the new power elite.

Generally speaking, the national leadership never took into account the evolution of social, economic, and historical imbalances between historically defined regions in a states. Rather, there was a slurred, romantic understanding of India's historical ethos, and it is understandable, though regrettable, that those in power were reluctant to relinquish control to those they considered inferior.

Parts of India are inhabited by "tribals" and so-called "hill people" who often are not part of the mainstream. They may live in particular regions of specific states. Such regions may demand a separate states if they feel discriminated against and deprived of development, and also if they feel that through resource transfers, others are prospering at their expense. This is what has happened in regions such as Marathawada, Vidarbha, and Konkan (in Maharashtra), Jharkhand (in Bihar), and Chhattisgarh (in Madhya Pradesh). The demands for statehood by tribal people in Jharkand, and by hill people in Uttaranchal, have been based on the perception that they have been victims of internal colonialism by other regional and cultural groups.

There are other parts of India that are quite prosperous. Here, a relatively rich region (in terms of resources or agricultural and industrial output) may resent having to support a backward region. An example of such a region is one in the more developed western part of the states of Uttar Pradesh, one that calls itself "Harit Pradesh."

The Historical Context

With hindsight, these problems might not have cropped up if, instead of the linguistic states' reorganization of 1956, the "rational reorganization" recommended by the Dar Commission's 1948 Report on the Linguistic Provinces had been widely accepted. That report stated: "Administrative convenience, history, geography, economy, culture and many other matters will have to be given due weight. It may be that the provinces thus formed will also show homogeneity of language and, in a way, might resemble linguistic provinces. But, in forming the provinces, the emphasis should be primarily on administrative convenience, and homogeneity of language will enter into consideration only as a matter of administrative convenience and not by its own independent force. [The Province] has to be financially self-supporting so as not to be a drag on the Centre for its subsistence. A new province cannot be forced by a majority upon a substantial minority of the people speaking the same language."[2]

To be fair, even the States' Reorganization Commission was in 1955 to recommend the creation of "sizeable-composite" states, with a self-sustaining economy. Right from the start, the emphasis was on political-economic viability rather than on linguistic homogeneity.[3] In 2000, Union Home Minister L.K. Advani said that the "Creation of new states was not the prescription for development, but experience showed that manageability and administrative viability were indeed 'big factors' in ensuring better governance and meeting aspirations of the people. The resolution by the states Assembly and economic viability were touchstones for creating new states. Though there was no constitutional bar on the Centre on creating new states, the government had decided to go ahead only if the state Assembly recommended and forwarded such proposal."[4]

The Union government did not willingly agree with the original reorganization of states on linguistic lines that took place in 1956. The appointment of the States' Reorganization Commission had come about only after much agitation. Even the commission itself did not make a very convincing case for linguistic reorganization, and the recommendations that it made appeared half-hearted. Many of the linguistic claims were not considered. In some instances, such as Punjab, proposals of the commission were not accepted. However, because of pressures from below, the reorganization of states on a linguistic basis was adopted and continued until the 1970s. After the linguistic reorganization, it did not take much time for demands to emerge from minorities in various regions for the creation of additional small states. The demands came from Andhra Pradesh (Telengana), Maharashtra (Vidharba and Marathwada), Assam (Bodoland), West Bengal (Gorkhaland), Jammu and Kashmir (Jammu and Ladakh), Guajrat (Saurashtra and Kutch), and Uttar Pradesh (Harit Pradesh and Bundelkhand). However, because of the emphasis on economic viability, not until 2000 were regions granted statehood because of their economic backwardness. That year saw the creation of Chhattisgarh, Jharkhand, and Uttaranchal.

"Internal Colonialism?"

Many of the demands for the formation of new states emanated from a perceived neglect, or what has been termed "internal colonialism." The essence of this argument is that the relationship between the dominant social group in a region and the peripheral groups-particularly those living in an identifiable territorial entity-was characterized by exploitation. The dominant group had acquired advantages over peripheral groups in the period of state-building, and then used this political-economic advantage to maintain and enhance its dominant position. The demand for a separate Telengana was a classic example of the argument against internal colonialism. Such an argument is more cogent if the ethnic group is not dispersed territorially. It can then readily perceive greater economic and political gains if it obtains greater regional autonomy. The demands for a separate Maharashtra out of greater Gujarat, and of Vidharba out of Maharashtra, reflect that phenomenon. Where greater regional autonomy, in the form of a separate states, is not a viable strategy or is perceived as not immediately possible, demands have been made for preferential treatment. The Telenganites in

Andhra Pradesh and the Shiv Sena, claiming to safeguard the interests of the Maharashtrans in the erstwhile Bombay, did just that. In both of these cases, there were fears among the native population of shrinking job markets (for Telengana's working and lower middle classes) and elsewhere of threats to the status of the middle classes (the Maharashtrans). The demand for a reorganization of the states of Assam was not based on language. Since the 1960s, the non-Assamese elite had perceived a direct status threat from the Assamese elite's attempts to make other ethnic groups accept the Assamese language. Similarly, the demands for Vidarbha, Marathawada, and Telengana were not based on language. The grievances expressed were economic in nature.

Thus, demands for separate states have emerged in areas that have experienced a rapid growth in the educational opportunities for the lower middle classes, enhancing their aspirations and expectations. However, these have not been fulfilled. Instead, there is a high level of unemployment among the indigenous middle classes. Moreover, migrants who are culturally alien may hold a substantial number of middle-class jobs. In such areas, the magnifying of cultural differences becomes a political technique, a way of defining cultural (and consequently, political) identity. The strategy has been to convert cultural differences into cultural, and thereby political, conflicts, thus emphasizing a distinct cultural identity that needs a separate territorial identity. Before articulating feelings of deprivation, a region has first to acquire an identity. It is the role of the political elite in such areas to construct a regional identity and then to point out the neglect and deprivation of the region because of being part of a bigger states. These groups, in almost all such demands for separate states, have tried to use political power to overcome economic subjugation and cultural subordination by the territorially dominant group.

It is a fact that most of the demands for constituting new states have been based primarily on an allegedly unfair and unequal distribution of development benefits and expenditures in multi-lingual "composite" states. If people have to live in the territory of the others, they may feel dominated.[5] The success of their demands is related to the success of the elite in marketing the perception of deprivation and in making what Benedict Anderson has termed an "imagined community" into a natural one.[6] Because numbers count in a democratic process, the forging of several identities into a common identity is politically expedient.

Jharkhand presents the best example of this phenomenon. Here, tribal cultural identities, combined with the backward developmental profile of the region, helped to forge a single distinct political identity. Over a period of more than a century, the movement for social and political equality was transformed into the movement for political freedom and, instead of a pan- tribal nature of ethnic identity, became a regional movement of tribal nationalism. By asserting that all tribals were members of the Jharkand party from birth, the Jharkhandi elite was successful in constructing a geographical identity that encompassed various cultural identities. However, it became clear that by geographically including all the residents of this region as Jharkhandis, the non-tribal people would benefit more, due to their educational and social advancement. The argument that was earlier given against a Jharkhand states was based on the minority status of the tribals spread over Bihar's neighboring states of Orissa, West Bengal, and Madhya Pradesh. Consequently, the move to broaden the base was abandoned by the Jharkhand elite. Even the demand for a separate states was put on the back burner. The flexible approach of the Jharkhand political elite became apparent when the Jharkhand party gave its support to the government of Bihar, led by the Rashtriya Janta Dal (RJD) party, in return for that party's support for a Jharkhand states. Earlier, the RJD and its allies were perceived as exploiters of the Jharkhand region. Now they were offering their support for the new states. Of course, it helped that in the process the RJD government acquired the support it needed to remain in office.

Regional Identity

Just as federal India is a composite, plural entity, so many states are based on plural identities. In European nation-states, linguistic homogeneity has often been the constitutional and legal basis of states formation and reorganization. But in India, the states are often simply cohesive political and administrative entities, based not on one identity but on a synthesis of different identities.

Among the states that do claim to have their own distinctive cultural identity are Assam, Mizoram, Nagaland, and Tripura, together with the three new states of Chhattisgarh, Uttaranchal, and Jharkhand. Each has its own traditions, dialects, and tribal and ethnic peculiarities. They are ecologically distinctive states. There also are states that claim to be ethnically distinctive. Among these are Tamil Nadu, Punjab, and Karnataka, based on language and dialect. Dravidian nationalism emanated from Tamil language and culture, and made Tamil Nadu a good example of an ethnically exclusive states. In another group of states, including West Bengal, Gujarat, Karnataka, Maharashtra, and Andhra Pradesh, regional identities have been subsumed under the dominant language, namely, Bengali, Gujarati, Kannada, Marathi, and Telegu. In other words, minorities in the regions remained "imagined communities," unable to create a common "we" in their region. All of these states are what may be called "single-identity states." It is in the large "composite" states like Bihar (with its tribals) and Uttar Pradesh (with its hill people in the Himalayan foothills) that the most demands have been made for new states. In the Jharkand region of Bihar, an attempt was made to create a distinctive cultural and linguistic identity for the region by creating a collective tribal consciousness of the Santhals, Mundaris, Hos, and Oraons.[7] However, because their contribution to a "Jharkhand identity" was not enough, non-tribal (Sadan) communities were included. Among the hill people in Uttar Pradesh are the Garhwalis and Kumaonis. These formed two distinct hill communities until a new regional identity of hill people was developed, making possible the new states of Uttaranchal. It remains to be seen whether this merger of identities will sustain the states as a cohesive political entity. Wherever there is non-congruence of the people and the states, there is cause for apprehension.

The Changing Politics of States' Reorganization

The reorganization of a states, or the formation of a new one, results from the political assertion of a regional community. In India, it is explained by a triangular relationship between the people, the territory, and the states.[8] There are numerous "eco-cultural" communities that have been identified[9] as having distinct identities within the 28 states and seven union territories. Some of these are identifiable socio-cultural regions that may be, or in some instances already are, the starting point of demands for further reorganization of states. On the basis of "maximum homogeneities within and maximum identity without," such regions reflect a set of variables: language or dialect, social composition of communities, ethnic regions, demographic features, area contiguity, cultural pattern, economy and economic life, historical antecedents, political background, and psychological make-up or felt consciousness of group identity. However, because the boundaries of these eco-cultural zones do not correspond with the administrative boundaries of states, there is always the possibility of forming new states and/or reorganizing the existing states. Some attempts to create commonalties of linguistic and political identities have not succeeded in erasing historical ethnic-regional identities, for example in Andhra Pradesh and Maharashtra. states may have been created, but "imagined communities" have yet to emerge.

Despite the claims of many states to be distinctive, only nine are culturally and administratively so compact that there are no demands for the creation of new states. These states are Arunachal Pradesh, Goa, Haryana, Himachal Pradesh, Kerala, Punjab, Sikkim, Tamil Nadu, and Tripura. By contrast, there are six large "composite" states (Andhra Pradesh, Bihar, Madhya Pradesh, Maharashtra, Rajasthan, and Uttar Pradesh). In these six states, there are 28 regional groups demanding new states.[11] These six are big, artificially created states, based on an imagined sense of identity; yet they lack the aforementioned variables of homogeneity. Their heterogeneity is presumed to have contributed to the lack of identification between the people and their states. It has led to demands for more states by people who question the legitimacy of composite states. A common language may not be enough. Linguistic identity in West Bengal alone has not precluded demands for separate states in Darjeeling-hills, Cooch-Bihar, Jalpaiguri, and Denajpur. Similarly, the recognition of linguistic states in the 1950s was not able to forestall the demand for a separate states of Telengana in Andhra Pradesh, or Vidharba-Marathwada in Maharashtra.

Is Re-organisation the Answer?

We have noted that demands for separate states develop when people of a region have the perception that they are deprived, discriminated against, and exploited by people from outside the region. However, it cannot be argued that such "discrimination" or "exploitation" disappears once a region becomes a states. Statehood may not lead to any perceptible difference in the condition of everyone, including those who may well have been the foot soldiers in the battle for a new states. The reorganization of states or the creation of a new states in the name of inequality or identity has often been driven by a regional elite that has hoped to displace the existing elite. Once successful in achieving the primary goal of coming to power, this elite may not necessarily be successful (or interested) in improving the condition of the people, generally, in providing a viable economy, or in promoting a more representative government. What has often happened has been simply the replacement of one elite by another. It is usually the better off among the "backwards" (as they are often called) who corner the advantages of development in the name of the other backwards and tribals.

It is questionable whether all sections and all groups within a states (even one ostensibly constituted as a uniform ethnic-linguistic entity) share the same values and the same concerns. The assumption of a new exclusive identity may exclude some peripheral identities, and this can make some people feel marginalized and deprived. This phenomenon is visible even in the recently formed states of Jharkhand and Chhattisgarh, where various tribes (Mundas, Santhals, Horos, and Orans) are not on the best of terms. Not everyone shares the dominant culture; therefore, there is always the possibility that such groups as Bengalis, Biharis, Marwaris, non-Santhals, and Christian tribals may feel discriminated against. Something similar happened in northeast India after the division of Assam into seven new states. Dissatisfaction continued among the Bodos, Deuris, and Misings in Assam; the Meitis and Kukis in Manipur; the Mizos, Chakmas, and Hmars in Mizoram; and the Garos, Khasis, and Jayantias in Meghalaya. In Sikkim, the Nepalis compete with the Lepcha-Bhotias. The expression of dissatisfaction by some groups often leads to similar reactions and demands by others, who may not even be in contiguous territories. The movement for separate states of Gorkhaland and Kamtapur in West Bengal got a boost from the formation of the three new states in 2000.

There is no reason to believe that the creation of a large number of small states will threaten the integrity and viability of the country. When the States' Reorganization Commission was constituted in the 1950s to find an acceptable basis for forming new states, it gave vent to the growing demands for regional autonomy from different parts of India. Although it accepted language as a basis, it was unable to provide an exclusive zone for every linguistic group.

A successful working of India's federal nation would involve administrative subdivision of the largest states on the principles of regional autonomy and regional identity. The large, composite states face problems of governance, and their very size may hamper economic development. Today's Uttar Pradesh, Bihar, Madhya Pradesh, and Rajasthan provide examples of states with problems. When the people are made partners in governance, the nation as such is strengthened. Evidence that political management, governance, and economic development are managed better in a smaller states is provided by the example of the states of Haryana, which until its creation in 1966 was a backward region of Punjab. Comparable development is possible elsewhere with the decentralization of power, and may lessen the demands for separate states. One should not rush to assume that granting more administrative and fiscal powers to the states, or creating a large number of states, would weaken the country.

Linguistic Homogeneity and Political Factors

Even after the reorganization of states on a linguistic basis, further demands for linguistic homogeneity emerged. These strengthened regionalism, both in terms of strength in unity and through emotional frenzy. On one hand are the positive examples of the creation of Maharashtra, Punjab, Haryana, and various states in the Northeast. On the other hand, there are the very different experiences of Telengana and Vidharba, where economic grievances and demands triumphed over linguistic homogeneity. The emotional commitment to language in a large states may get sidelined when it is perceived that the demographic, cultural, and economic balance is being upset by an ailing regional economy. The assertion of a regional identity may be based on a common history of grievances emanating from an underdeveloped regional economy.

A number of regions have identities based not on language but on dialect. Among them are Bundelkhand, Braj, Bhojpur, Oudh, and Rohilkhand in Uttar Pradesh; Malwa and Mahakoshal in Madhya Pradesh; Maithal in Bihar; and Konkan in Maharashtra. All of them have an identity based on dialect, and yet they are economically and administratively viable. These regions now have the same grievances, and the same aspirations, which the earlier regions based on linguistic identities had shown. However, the target of their grievances is not so much the Center as the states of which they are a part. In some cases, as in Uttaranchal, the Center may even be perceived as sympathetic because it was instrumental in the creation of the states.

It would be interesting to find out who is demanding the reorganization of big states, like Uttar Pradesh. There is a view that such demands emanate from "outside" forces apprehensive of the large number of members that a big states sends to Parliament.

India's states were constituted for various reasons, only one of which was linguistic homogeneity. As pointed out by Rasheeduddin Khan: "Together with language, many variables and critical factors like ethnic-cum-economic considerations (Nagaland, Meghalaya, Manipur and Tripura); religion-script and sentiments (Haryana and Punjab); language-cum-culture (Maharashtra and Gujarat); historical and political factors (Uttar Pradesh and Bihar); integration of princely states and the need for viable groupings (Madhya Pradesh and Rajasthan); and, of course, language-cum-social distinctiveness (Tamil Nadu, Kerala, Mysore, Bengal and Orissa) have played a decisive role in the composition of the Indian federation."[12]

The experience of the three states constituted in 2000 is interesting. The demand for a separate states of Chhattisgarh started in the 1950s. The region is culturally distinctive. However, the people who started and sustained the demand for a separate states were the rich peasants, those who had long managed the local affairs of the former rulers, from the Marathas to the British. Traditionally, this group supported the Congress party, and it was the Congress party that first came to power in the new states. For Uttaranchal, it was the region's ecology-based ethnic identity, defined in terms of lack of development in the hills, which became the basis of the demand for a separate states. The successive governments of Uttar Pradesh, of various political parties, were blamed for the developmental neglect of the Uttaranchal region. When the new states was formed, the government of Uttar Pradesh was of the Bhartiya Janata Party (BJP). Since at that time the BJP's government in the states was identified with the economic backwardness of Uttaranchal, it was the Congress party that succeeded in forming the government. Caste also played a part. In the unified Uttar Pradesh, the upper castes did not constitute a numerical majority, whereas in Uttaranchal they did. They formed a traditional support group of the Congress party, which benefited electorally from the formation of the new states. In Jharkhand, the third new states, the political elite was for long marginalized and had tried to align with different political parties. The leaders then decided to disrupt the Jharkand economy. At this point, the national political parties started taking them seriously. Because the Bhartiya Janata Party threw its weight behind the demand for a separate states, support for that option grew steadily in the Jharkhand region. The BJP adopted the earlier position of the Jharkhand Party and forged a geographical identity encompassing both the tribal and non-tribal groups of the region. It asserted that the large size of a states like Bihar was detrimental to its development prospects, and was successful in arguing that the backwardness of the region was the result of poor governance. The BJP's electoral platform promised quality governance in place of poor management and inefficient.

Many of the demands for new states have been due to disagreements among the undivided state's ruling elite. The regional elite has asserted itself against the states elite, claiming that economic backwardness is a result of the region's political underrepresentation. The demand for new states in many undivided states has reflected dissatisfaction with the ruling elite. A similar situation has occurred in the Northeast: the demand for Bodoland in Assam, for

Goroland in Meghalaya, for Kukiland in Nagaland, and for a Hamar states in Mizoram. All of them reflect the dissatisfaction of the regional elite with the existing power-distribution structure. The regional leaders have demanded a framework whereby powers are divided between states and region. Political factors rather than rationality often determine the nature of a new states. In Uttaranchal, ethnic, cultural, linguistic, or historical homogeneity was not taken into account when the district of Udham Singh Nagar was made part of the states. The district was a predominantly Punjabi-speaking Sikh area that wanted to remain in Uttar Pradesh to further Sikh business interests. However, in order to make the new states economically viable, this region was incorporated into Uttaranchal, thus creating among the Sikhs a feeling of being exploited by the "others."

Such a perception was not peculiar to Uttaranchal. In all three of the new states, the principle of natural and social homogeneity was not adhered to fully. Perceptions persist that there remained some territories, in adjacent states, that should have been transferred to the new states on the principles of compactness and homogeneity. Consequently, it was perceived that states formation was based not on objective considerations but because of political and electoral compulsions. Such a perception is not altogether unfounded. In the creation of new states, there has been no uniform principle and no clear and open practice.

During the 1950s, the approach was to accept the linguistic demands for separate states and therefore speakers of languages such as Assamese, Bengali, Gujarati, Kashmiri, Kannada, Malayalam, Marathi, Punjabi, Telugu, and Tamil were awarded separate states. At that time, similar claims by smaller communities, such as those who spoke Konkani, Bhojpuri, and Maithili, were not recognized. At a later stage, the administrative and financial viability of the new entity became the decisive criteria. These considerations were, however, disregarded when the Northeast was reorganized, creating seven states on the basis of ethnic considerations. But ethnic considerations were not taken into account when large "composite" states were formed, such as Uttar Pradesh, Madhya Pradesh, Rajasthan, and Bihar. Here, the basis of a presumed "homogeneity" was sought in the interaction of history and the region's resources. If we consider the size of these four states (together with Andhra Pradesh and Maharashtra) and compare them with tiny Goa, Sikkim, and Tripura, we find no uniformity. In Mizoram and Meghalaya, the district councils evolved into new states, but not elsewhere. In different situations, different factors have played the decisive role in states formation. In some, the political elite and governing parties have not been in favor of, or have been opposed to, the formation of new states. They have acted according to their own interests.[13] Elsewhere ethnic minorities have established a territorial identity (as in Assam, Maharashtra, Telegana, Punjab, Jharkhand, and Nagaland). Culture has been made not just an instrument for, but also a source of, revivalism and chauvinism. In all of these situations, the elite has attempted mobilization of people fearful of threats to "our" culture from "them." This perception of a threat to culture has been used as a political weapon by the entrenched elite to defend its privileges. In all the movements asking for the creation of new states, the underprivileged have been in the vanguard, fighting street battles. What are actually being defended are the privileges of the elite.

What has been often overlooked, in the formation of new states, is not just the economic viability of the new states (as in Uttaranchal) but also the overall economic repercussions for the truncated states. For instance, when

Jharkhand was created, it consisted of 18 sparsely populated districts of Bihar, together with their mines and commercial taxes. The 65 percent of the population that remained in undivided Bihar suffered a tremendous revenue loss. Few new states have the resources of Jharkand. It is not just Uttaranchal that lacks sustaining resources; many other small states do not have adequate infrastructure for development. If the economy is neither self-sustaining nor growth-oriented, the states is not in a position to meet the socioeconomic expectations of the very people for whom it was formed. Sikkim, Arunachal Pradesh, Nagaland, and Tripura seem to share this situation with Uttaranchal. When the viability of states like Uttaranchal and Chhattisgarh is questioned, the only explanation that comes to mind for their formation is the dubious political gain for the elite of these regions. What should have been done, instead of a simple division of assets and liabilities, was the laying down of policy guidelines for the economic development of both the new and the truncated states.

The Change in Outlook

The creation of the three new states (Chhattisgarh, Jharkhand, and Uttaranchal) in 2000, and Telengana in 2009, signified a change in the thinking of the Union. For nearly four decades, the union government and virtually all the political parties had resisted the creation of new states, and these came into existence only after much bickering and pressure. Sometimes, a party would support the demand for a states using arguments it would reject elsewhere. Sometimes the regional leadership of a party supported a demand while the national party opposed it. On the whole, reorganization of states was not considered "normal" political activity and so debate over the issue was generally avoided. The states formation in 2000 became a milestone when the issue became a normal and permissible theme of party agendas and of mainstream political activity. The demand was not treated as a threat to national integration and security (even though one of the states was on an international border). There were no mass movements. The union did not drag its feet. Further, these states were proposed and created not on a linguistic basis but on the basis of regional identity enshrined in cultural and geographical differences. The justification for these states was administrative efficiency. It was argued that the parent states (Bihar, Uttar Pradesh, and Madhya Pradesh) were too big and hence difficult to administer well, whereas states like Haryana could develop because their small size made administration efficient. On all counts, there was a qualitative shift in political attitudes (though the arguments in favor of states formation may not have been convincing).

There appears to have been a change in the thinking of national leaders regarding the territorial demands of linguistic identities. They recognize that cohesive linguistic groups do aspire to political union and that it is better to give them some autonomous existence in a federation. The aim is supposedly the development of linguistic and cultural diversity. Yet, there may be a lurking suspicion that political identities based on language generate forces that are a threat to national unity. As a result of this residual suspicion, a certain bitterness persists in the new states, even after achieving their goals. Territorial identity may have been constitutionally recognized in order to contain regional identities within the confines of a political formula. Consequently, any demand for a new states, or even any manifestation of regionalism, is suspected of being anti-system. The reorganization of the states was important because it made possible the emergence of a new elite. Its members had enjoyed leadership in rural India but had been denied representation at the states level. Now they entered the political and administrative structure and, thus, got a voice and a stake in the political affairs of the states. If anything, this only strengthened and consolidated India as a multicultural states.

These "durable entities" are based on commonality of culture. In India, the emergence of both a states and regional identity and the struggle for their achievement have been simultaneous. A consciousness of being separate has motivated those in the struggle, and out of the struggle has emerged a new consciousness. There are now 30 more demands for new states. It is time for the states to be reorganized in a manner that accommodates and institutionalizes the various regional identities. One way could be to identify the four bases for reorganization referred to earlier: administrative convenience, economic viability, similarity in the developmental needs of the region, and cultural, linguistic affinity. On this basis, even if more states are formed, it would only be strengthening the "self-rule, shared-rule" principle of federal governance. Alternatively, in many cases, formation of new states may not be rational and, therefore, some degree of regional autonomy might be a better solution, and that might provide quality governance, as well.

Notes

1. R.D. King has discussed this at length in his *Nehru and the Language Politics of India*, (New Delhi: Oxford University Press, 1997). See also Selig Harrison, *India: The Most Dangerous Decades*, (Princeton, NJ: Princeton University Press, 1960).
2. B. Shiva Rao, *The Framing of India's Constitution: Select Documents*, (New Delhi: Indian Institute of Public Administration, 1968), pp. 443 and 475.

3. The Nehru Committee Report, 1928; Report of the Linguistic Provinces Commission (Dar Report), 1948; White Paper on Indian states, 1950; States' Reorganization Commission, 1955.
4. "Chattisgarh Bill Okayed," *The Hindu*, 10 August 2000, http://www.hinduonnet.com/thehindu/2000/ 08/10/stories/0110000b.htm
5. Javed Alam, *India: Living With Modernity*, (New Delhi: Oxford University Press, 1999), p. 160.
6. Benedict Anderson, *Imagined Communities: Reflections on the Origin and Spread of Nationalism*, (London: Verso, 1983).
7. A.K. Singh, "Jharkhand Movement," *Rethinking Indian Federalism*, ed., R. Khan (Shimla: IIAS, 1997), pp. 241-252.
8. Ajay Kumar Singh, "Sub Regions," *Constitutional Nation Building: Half a Century of India's Success*, (ed.), Akhtar Majeed (New Delhi: Manak Publications, 2001), p. 121.
9. S. Singh, "Introduction," *National Series*, Vol. IV: India's Communities (New Delhi: Oxford University Press, 1998), mentions 96 such zones.
10. Rasheeduddin Khan, *Federal India: A Design for Change*, (New Delhi: Vikas, 1992), p. 109.
11. Demands for creation of more states out of these six states are/have been: (1) Andhra Pradesh: Telengana, Andhra, Rayal Seema; (2) Bihar: Jharkhand (demand achieved), Mithila, Magadh; (3) Madhya Pradesh: Chhattisgarh (demand achieved), Malwa, Dandkarnia, Bhilistan, Baghelkhand; (4) Maharashtra: Konkan, Khandesh, Marathwada, Vidharba; (5) Rajasthan: Mewar, Marwar, Mewat Aravallis; and (6) Uttar Pradesh: Uttaranchal (demand achieved), Bundelkhand, Braj, Oudh, Harit Pradesh, Rohilkhand, Bhojpur, Poorvanchal.
12. Rasheeduddin Khan, "Territorial Reorganization," *Seminar*, 137 (January 1971): 28-32.
13. J.A. Schlesinger, "Party Units," *International Encyclopaedia of the Social Sciences*, (New York: Macmillan, 1968), Volume II, p. 430. Like Haryana and Kerala, Sikkim and many other states in the Northeast are also small in size but not as developed or as efficient administratively. Andhra Pradesh, Tamil Nadu,

and Karnataka are not small in size but pretty well developed and well administered, unlike other big states like Uttar Pradesh and Bihar. May be the perceived political gains had something to do with this, though many of the calculations of many political parties and groups misfired.

4

Working of the Indian Federal System

As a Governance-Mechanism, Federalism combines unity with diversity, linking self-rule with shared-rule. This involves creating or preserving two levels of government, each with a direct relationship with the people, and by dividing power between them. In this system, unity is achieved through the exercise of power by the central government, in relation to all the people. Diversity comes through the exercise of power by constituent governments representing sections of the people, generally territorially identified. The boundaries of power between the two spheres of government are protected by a written constitution, which is interpreted and applied by a court or courts.

Federal states are also seen as tending to aggravate problems with co-ordinating policy objectives, generating competency overlap and competition among the different levels of government, given the negative relation between dispersion of political authority and internal consistency of collective decisions. However, concentration of political authority varies among federal states, depending on the way relations between the executive and the legislative branches of government are structured at the federal level, and varies among policies, depending on how intergovernmental relations are structured in regard to specific policies.

Functional federalism relies upon an effective structure or mechanism, and a commitment to using those structures on a regular and frequent basis. In this system, liberty is safe because power is divided to maximum, there are a number of checks and balances, there is Separation of Executive and Legislative power, there is a distribution of functions and powers between sets of governments, and there are "States' rights" vs. Central government

Whatever the theory, it is neither possible nor, in some cases, desirable for member governments in a federal polity to exercise their powers entirely in isolation from each other. However carefully powers are allocated between the spheres of government, substantial interaction and co-operation is inevitable, because of the complexity of social organisation, increased economic integration, and the exigencies of politics. Now, the phenomenon of co-operation has increased, in response to the pressures of globalisation, and, often, the inflexibility of formal federal constitutions.

Though only 25 of the world's 193 countries have federal political systems, their citizens make up 40 per cent of the world's population:

1. Argentina
2. Australia
3. Austria
4. Belgium
5. Bosnia and Herzegovina
6. Brazil
7. Canada
8. Comoros

9. Ethiopia
10. Germany
11. India
12. Malaysia
13. Mexico
14. Micronesia
15. Nigeria
16. Pakistan
17. Russia
18. St. Kitts and Nevis
19. Serbia and Montenegro
20. South Africa
21. Spain
22. Switzerland
23. Sudan
24. United Arab Emirates
25. United States of America
26. Venezuela

Source: Handbook of Federal Countries: 2002, Montreal and Kingston: McGill-Queen's University Press, 2002.

A country the size of a continent, with an area of 12,65 000 sq. miles and the population of over a Billion, India is the most extreme plural society with 22 national languages and some 2000 dialects, a dozen ethnic and seven religious groups fragmented into a large number of sects, castes and sub-castes, and some sixty socio-cultural sub-regions spread over seven natural geographic regions. This "Union of states" has 29 states and six Union territories' as units of federation.

The largest written one, the Constitution of India has 395 Articles (divided into 22 parts), 12 schedules and 3 appendices, and is, in fact, a detailed legal code dealing with all important aspects of the constitutional and administrative system of the country in which: (a)—the powers of the Executive, Legislative and Judiciary are defined and none can act beyond its powers so defined, (b)—it is with reference to the fundamental law that the validity of the laws enacted by the Legislature is to be tested, (c)—the Judiciary is the guardian of the Constitution. The Constitution is generally flexible but rigid in 'federal' matters, and any change in the federal provisions requires a special majority in Parliament as also ratification by at least half of the Legislatures of the states.

The purpose of the Constitution is to identify the sources of the constitutional authority and the objectives that it seeks to establish and promote. The Objectives Resolution of the Constituent Assembly (22 January 1947) had declared that all powers and authority of the Sovereign Independent India, its constituent units and organs of government are derived from the people, and adequate safeguards shall be provided for minorities, backward and tribal areas and depressed and other backward classes. The Preamble lays down the Objective to constitute India into "a sovereign, socialist, Secular, Democratic Republic" and to secure to all the citizens Justice, liberty, equality and fraternity. Socialism aims at eliminating inequality and exploitation and to provide a decent standard of life to the citizens of a welfare states. The Preamble to the Constitution specifies certain objectives that reflect the basic structure of the Indian Constitution and that cannot be amended. Some of the basic features of the Constitution that cannot be altered or destroyed are: The Supremacy of the Constitution, the Republican form of government, the democratic form of life, as distinct from mere adult franchise, guaranteeing fundamental rights, the secular nature of states in which there is no states religion, a free and independent judiciary, and a balance between the legislature, the executive and the judiciary, and the federal system of governance.

Various innovative terms have been used to describe Indian federalism, unitary, cooperative, executive, parliamentary, centralist, restructured, reluctant, competitive, etc. A curious phenomenon is that we tend to read into our Constitution provisions that do not exist and overlook those provisions that may not be to our liking at some particular time. There is a tendency to forget that our federal system is a device of shared-governance, for sharing power in our social-pluralism that is territorially identified.

In most of the contemporary states and societies, certain federal practices can be instruments not just of good governance but also of conflict management. They include power-sharing, people's participation, devolution of power and authority, and inter-governmental collaboration. This is particularly so in plural societies— that form an overwhelming majority in the international community. In such societies, issues of unity with diversity, self-rule and peaceful resolution of contentious issues, between tiers of government, have attracted attention and growing interest of scholars and practitioners of federalism.

The Indian federal Union was formed to (1) put in place a mechanism of federal governance with a strong parliamentary centre, (2) guarantee cultural autonomy to regions with strong linguistic, religious, tribal, and/or territorial identities, (3) create a mixed economy with sectors demarcated for states and private enterprise, and (4) reduce regional and economic disparities through fiscal federalism and planning.

Given that the Union is not the result of any agreement between the states, there is no concept of equality of states' rights and, consequently, no equality of representation of states in the Council of states (the second chamber of the Union Parliament). The second chamber is thus not a "federal" chamber. The states cannot claim any inviolability as regards their territory, boundaries, area, or even name.

The following provisions of the Constitution fall under the category where, after being passed by a two-third's majority in the Parliament, a ratification by at least half of the states Assemblies is also required, for a Constitutional amendment: (1) election of the President (Art. 57), (2) extent of the executive power of the Union (Art. 73), (3) extent of the executive power of the states (Art. 162), (4) the Union judiciary (Ch. IV of Prt V), (5) high courts in the states (Ch. V of Prt VI), (6) any of the lists in the Seventh Schedule, (7) the representation of states in Parliament, and (8) provisions dealing with amendment of the Constitution.

India's Constitution is not a covenant, or compact, between the states; rather, the states are the creation of the Constitution and subsequently of Parliament. Consequently, the states do not have an inherent right to share in the amending process, except insofar as the Constitution provides for states legislative participation in the matters listed above — all of which impinge significantly upon the states.

The position of the states under the Indian Constitution can be summed up as follows:

(i) The Constitution does not grant to any states the right of secession.

(ii) The states do not have any *a priori* rights, but only such rights as have been expressly granted to them by the Constitution. Even the residuary rights vest in the Union Government. In the concurrent field of powers it is the Union law which prevails over a state law in the event of a conflict between the two.

(iii) There is a single Constitution both for the Union and the states.

(iv) There is a single unified Judiciary for the whole country and an integrated Civil Service under the supervision and control of the All Indian Services.

(v) There is a single Citizenship for the people of the country and no separate Citizenship for the people of any states.

(vi) The Governors of states are appointees of the Union Government and besides being the constitutional head of the states are also the eyes and ears of the Union in the states.

(vii) The Constitution guarantees individual rights and rights of certain groups, such as scheduled castes, scheduled tribes, and minorities, but not of states as such. It does not concede even the right of equal representation to the states in the Upper House of the Union Parliament.

Actually, in view of historical traditions of centralisation of power and authority, the operative principle in the making of India's Constitution was that a government was best when it was able to bring about social transformation. Hence, the framers of our Constitution and the subsequent law-makers consciously ensured that the overwhelming majority of powers and authority was kept with the Union government

The executive power of the Union extends to giving of such directions to a states as may appear to be necessary for that purpose. However, this does not empower the Union to interfere in any matter pertaining to the exclusive concern of a states. The Union can issue a direction only where some action of a states government is likely to prejudice the exercise of the executive power of the Union, with the Constitution. In cases of matters falling within states jurisdiction, like the maintenance of law and order, Art. 257(1) cannot be applied.

The power of the Union government to give directions to the states governments is fortified by provisions of Art. 365. Constitutional breakdown occurs when a government resigns following its defeat in the legislature and no alternative ministry, enjoying the support of the legislature, can be formed; when even a coalition government is not possible when the majority party refuses to form a government; when the states government fails to carry out the directions of the Union government; when the states executive flouts the judgement of the Court that may have declared a states law as unconstitutional; when the states executive does not obey the directions of the states legislature; when normal legislative procedure is paralysed by the members or otherwise; when the states government has no control over the administrative and civil service of the states; and when the states government seeks to use its constitutional powers for purposes not authorised by the Constitution and does not heed to warnings or other corrective measures. However, in the light of the Supreme Court judgement in the Bommai case (1994), it is clear that the directions given by the Union executive should be lawful and that states's failure to comply with them should lead to a situation where governance according to Constitution (Art. 356-I) was not possible. It is clear that the use of Art. 356 is to be made in cases of emergency.

The Constitution regulates in elaborate detail the legislative and administrative relations between the Union and the states as well as the distribution of revenues between them. The outcome is that the Union is invested with wider jurisdiction for the operation of its legislative and executive authority than are most other federal systems. The residual powers, as in Canada but unlike in the United States and Switzerland, are vested in the Union.

The primacy of the Union over the states in the

legislative field is carried over into the administrative arena as well, the basic constitutional premise being that the executive power is co-extensive with the legislative power.

The Constitution directs that the executive power of every states be so exercised as to ensure compliance with, and not to impede or prejudice, the exercise of the executive power of the Union, and the Union has the power to give such directions to a states as may appear necessary for the purpose of ensuring compliance with Union laws (Art. 256). However, the Supreme Court has held that this does not empower the Union to interfere in any matter pertaining to the exclusive concern of a states.

The Constitution establishes a rather centralised polity in which the Union government is vested with sufficient powers to ensure not only its dominance, but also its ability to rule in a unitary fashion, if necessary, and politically feasible. Equally important, the country's diversity and socio-economic conditions, coupled with the ideological influences of socialism, drove the Constitution toward a kind of organically unitary federalism in the name of justice, equality, and rights protection.

There is a Third-Tier of Indian federal structure, comprised of Local-governing bodies. Part IX of the Constitution outlines the framework of institutions of rural self-government: a three-tier system of units known, in ascending order, as the village, intermediate, and district *panchayats*. The Panchayati Raj system came into existence with two basic objectives: (a) democratic decentralisation and (b) local participation in planned programmes.

Part IXA of the Constitution sets forth the framework of urban local government. Three types of institutions of local self-government have been provided for urban areas, namely *nagar panchayats* for transitional areas (i.e., areas that are being transformed from rural to urban), municipal councils for small urban areas, and municipal corporations for large urban areas. Every states is obliged to constitute such units. Local government remains an exclusive states subject. The Seventy-Third and Seventy-Fourth Amendments outline the scheme by which the states can bring their laws on local government into conformity with these amendments.The Constitution provides for direct election of local bodies, in urban and rural areas, every five years. The other noticeable provisions are:

(i) reservation of seats for women and for scheduled castes and tribes.
(ii) a states Finance Commission to ensure financial viability of these institutions.
(iii) devolution of powers and responsibilities to the local bodies with respect to:
    (a) preparation of plans and implementation of schemes for economic development and social justice.
    (b) devolution of financial powers to the local bodies,
    (c) endowment of these institutions with powers, authority and responsibility to prepare plans for economic development and community welfare programmes for revenue raising responsibilities.

The Statements of Objects and Reasons made at the time of introduction of 73rd & 74th amendment bills discussed the reasons of local bodies having become weak and not able to perform effectively as vibrant democratic units of self-government, and three facts were identified, among a variety of reasons that hold good in case of many states: (i) the failure of holding regular elections, (ii) prolonged supersessions, and (iii) inadequate devolution of powers and functions. The amendment sought to (a) put on a firmer footing the relationship between a states government and its local bodies with regard to the functions and taxation powers and arrangement for revenue sharing, (b) ensure regular conduct of election and timely elections in case of supersession, and (c) provide adequate representation for weaker sections like scheduled castes, scheduled tribes and women.

Constitutions's Art. 243G and 243W stipulate that the Legislature of a states may, by law, endow the panchayats / municipalities with such powers and authority as may be necessary to enable them to function as institutions of self-government and further suggest that such law may contain provision for the devolution of power and responsibilities upon pachayats / municipalities—subject to such conditions as may be specified—with respect to (i) the preparation of plans for economic development and social justice and (ii) the performance of functions and the implementation of schemes as may be entrusted to them including those in relation to the matter listed in the Eleventh & Twelfth Schedule. Art. 243R also suggests that the Legislature of a states may, by law, endow the Committees (the Wards Committees) with such powers and authority as may be necessary to enable them to carry out the responsibilities conferred upon them including those in relation to the matters listed in the Twelfth Schedule. Panchayats have now been given powers and responsibilities to making plans for economic development, social justice and the implementation of schemes listed in the Eleventh Schedule. These activities include: anti-poverty programmes, such as Integrated Rural Development Programme, land improvement, minor irrigation, social forestry, small scale and cottage industry; Primary and Secondary Schools, non-formal education, technical training; health and sanitation and family welfare; social welfare, welfare of weaker sections, public distribution system and women and child development; roads, housing, drinking water, markets, electrification, maintenance of community assets etc.

Many states have delegated functions to local bodies through executive orders rather than transfers through legislation. They can be thus withdrawn with ease. Even if they are not formally withdrawn, they can be made ineffective by instituting boards and authorities for local functions like Development Authorities (practically in all municipal corporations) and Special Purpose Authorities which came much at the wishes of the World Bank and World Health Organisation, for example in water supply and even in sanitation and drainage. While the representatives of local governments were not consulted in procurement of loans or in preparation and execution of the schemes by their respective states governments, the loan liability was passed on to the local government under the presumption that it is a basically a civic function. Of late, due to resentment of elected civic bodies, some of these functions have been restored to local bodies and functionaries are put under the control of the local elected authorities.

In most of the cases, the role of panchayats has been reduced to that of agencies of states government meant to implement various development programmes and schemes. Inspite of that, though the overall progress of decentralization is slow, the mobilization at the grass-root levels is working to the advantage of women and backward sections of society.

After the states Reorganisation Act 1956, five Zonal Councils were set up, each composed of the chief ministers of the states in a council's zone, the development ministers and chief secretaries of these states, and a member of the Planning Commission, with each council headed by the Union's home minister. The zonal councils were intended to foster the psychological integration of the country by mitigating regional consciousness; helping the Union and states governments to evolve uniform social and economic policies; assisting with effective implementation of development projects; and evolving a degree of political equilibrium among the regions of the country. Regarding the Autonomous District Councils, the National Commission to Review the Working of the Constitution had observed that: "The subjects given under the Sixth Schedule and those mentioned in the Eleventh Schedule could be entrusted to the Autonomous District Councils (ADCs). The system of in-built safeguards in the Sixth Schedule should be maintained and strengthened for the minority and micro-minority groups while empowering them with greater responsibilities and opportunities, for example, through the process of Central funding for Plan expenditure instead of routing all funds through the states governments. The North-Eastern Council can play a central role here by developing a process of public education on the proposed changes, which would assure communities about protection of their traditions and also bring in gender representation and give voice to other ethnic groups."

The division of powers between the Union and the states reflects the distribution of responsibilities between them. The Union has been assigned the duty of nation building, maintenance of unity, protection of territorial integrity of the country, and maintenance of constitutional-political order throughout the country. The states are to cooperate with the Union in performing these functions and in discharging their own constitutional duties with regard to local issues. But as soon as any subject ceases to be "local," the Union may intervene to legislate on the matter. *The {Sarkaria} Commission on Centre-states Relations* (1988) was set up to examine the working of the arrangements between the Centre and the states and recommend such changes in the said arrangements as may be appropriate within the present constitutional framework. The report of the Commission had noted that the mechanism of inter-governmental relations in India were tilted in favour of the Central government with the result that there is "blood pressure at the Centre and anemia at the periphery," resulting in morbidity and inefficiency.

In the federal scheme of things, distribution of responsibilities is tilted in favour of the Union government. First, the Union has exclusive power to legislate on the 97 subjects in the Union List and concurrent power to legislate on the 47 subjects in the Concurrent List. Second, although the Union shares with the states the power to legislate on subjects in the Concurrent List, Union law has priority over any states law in the event of a conflict between the two. Third, the residual powers, as in Canada but unlike in the United States and Switzerland, are vested in the Union. Fourth, the Union Parliament can make laws on subjects in the States List if (1) the *Rajya Sabha* (upper chamber of Parliament), by a resolution passed by not less than two-thirds of the members present and voting, declares that it is expedient or necessary, as a matter of national interest, to do so (Art. 249); (2) a proclamation of national emergency is in operation (Art. 250); (3) the legislatures of one or more states pass resolutions to that effect (Art. 252); or (4) the Union law is to give effect to "any treaty, agreement or convention with any other country or countries or any decision made at any international conference, association or other body" (Art. 253). In this way, the Union may legislate in the field of the states in specified circumstances.

The sharing of powers between the Union government and the states governments has come to a situation in which the former has what powers it had but shares in the powers that the latter had. Consequently, what evolved was as if Union's powers were exclusive powers and states' powers were shared powers.

In many of the spheres of states activity, the Central government has stepped in not through any constitutional provision but through the process of administration. In matters of implementation of plan policies in areas of land-reforms, forest development, development of rural industries, irrigation, cooperative farming, agriculture, education, health, cottage industries etc, the Planning Commission insists on uniform policies to be followed by the states. It is believed that though the primary responsibility in such matters is of states governments, the Centre has an overall responsibility for helping coordinate and guide the work of the states so that national policies can be satisfactorily worked out. Entry 20 of the Concurrent List (VIIth Schedule) of the Constitution empowers both the Centre and the states to legislate on economic and social planning, and there are a number of subjects in the States' list which are relevant to planning. Since the central law prevails in the event of jurisdiction dispute between the Centre and the states, the Centre can go to any extent in the name of planning.

However, the wide powers given to the Union under List I and III, and limited powers given to the states in List II, must not be seen in terms of "either-or-federalism" of the past, which rested on a dichotomy between the Centre and the states. The two should not be seen as competing centers of power but as co-partners in the task of nation building.

Union-states cooperation, as worded in Part XI of the

Constitution, leaves ample scope for conflict over interpretation of definitional phrases such as "national interest" and "Union's direction." Article 263, therefore, allows the president to establish an *Inter-states Council* (ISC) to work out modalities for continuing cooperation and to forge procedures for coordination between the Union and the states as well as among the states themselves. The text of Article 263 is so phrased as to allow the council to discuss, debate, and recommend suitable policy measures on any subject, whether characterised as "national" or as "public." There is scope for enlarging the ambit of the council, as it would be lawful for a presidential order "to define the nature of the duties to be performed by it and its organisation and procedure." As an advisory body, the council may inquire into disputes that "have arisen between states"; investigate and discuss subjects "in which some or all of the states, or the Union and one or more of the states, have a common interest"; or recommend better coordination of policy and action on any subject necessitating interaction between the Union and the states. Since the ISC is an advisory body, it is difficult to assess the efficacy of its policy performance. With the Central government becoming weak..... different political parties ruling at the Centre and in several states, and the Central government enjoying the majority support in the Parliament without the party being in majority..... and due to exigencies of coalition politics, the Central governments had to share power. The bargaining power of the states with the Centre has markedly increased and they no longer need a mechanism like the ISC to bargain with the Centre.

The Constitution regulates in elaborate detail the legislative and administrative relations between the Union and the states as well as the distribution of revenues between them. The outcome is that the Union is invested with wider jurisdiction for the operation of its legislative and executive authority than are most other federal systems.

The primacy of the Union over the states in the legislative field is carried over into the administrative arena as well, the basic constitutional premise being that the executive power is co-extensive with the legislative power.

The Union government can acquire the features of a unitary system in an emergency, in which case its legislative power extends to states subjects. Even in normal circumstances, the Council of states can, by a two-thirds vote, transfer a subject from the States List to the Union List if such legislation is necessary for the "national interest." There is likewise a kind of paramountcy of the Union in provisions for the suspension of states governments and the imposition of President's Rule. However, all of the foregoing does not mean that states are mere appendages of the Union. In the sphere allotted to them, the states are supreme and have an independent constitutional existence. The Constitution is in the nature of a covenant among the people as such, and the states are the creation of this Constitution.

The Constitution directs that the executive power of every states be so exercised as to ensure compliance with, and not to impede or prejudice, the exercise of the executive power of the Union, and the Union has the power to give such directions to a states as may appear necessary for the purpose of ensuring compliance with Union laws (Art. 256). However, the Supreme Court has held that this does not empower the Union to interfere in any matter pertaining to the exclusive concern of a states. Article 256 of the Constitution lays down that "the executive power of every states shall be exercised as to ensure compliance with the laws made by Parliament and any existing laws which apply in that states and the executive power of the Union shall extend to giving of such directions to a states as may appear to the Government of India to be necessary for that purpose." However, the Supreme Court, {in the *states of Rajasthan Vs Union of India*, 1979} held that this does not empower the Union to interfere in any matter pertaining to the exclusive concern of a states and if the Prime Minister issues any directive to a states in the exclusive states sphere, such directive shall not be binding upon the states. However, Art. 257(1) elaborates that "the executive power of the Union shall extend to the giving of such directions to a states as may appear to the Government of India to be necessary for that purpose." The Court held that it was rather obvious that, under this provision, the Union can issue a direction only where some action of a states government is likely to prejudice the exercise of the executive power of the Union. In cases of matters falling within states jurisdiction, like the maintenance of law and order, Art. 257(1) cannot be applied.

Under article 356, the President may by proclamation assume to himself the executive powers of the states and declare that the powers of the states legislature shall be exercised by or under the authority of the Union Parliament. When a proclamation of emergency is in operation, the Union executive is empowered to give directions to any states on how the executive power thereof is to be exercised.

However, in a 1994 judgement having far-reaching consequences, the Supreme Court held that the Court can examine whether the president issued a proclamation based on bad faith *(mala fides)* or on irrelevant considerations because the Court is not precluded from calling upon the Union government to disclose to the Court the material upon which the president formed his or her judgement. The Supreme Court in this case laid down following main propositions in regard to use of Article 356:

(a) Presidential proclamation dissolving a states Legislative Assembly is subject to judicial review;
(b) burden lies on the Union Government to prove that relevant material existed to justify the issue of proclamation; and
(c) having regard to the overall constitutional scheme, the President shall exercise the power of dissolving the Legislative Assembly, only after the Proclamation is approved by both Houses of Parliament and until such approval, the Assembly should be kept under suspended animation.

In this way, the Court sought to contain the Union government's attempts to ride roughshod over the states by threatening them with dismissal.

The National Commission to Review the Working of the Constitution (2002) recommended: (i) greater consultation between the Union and the states through the Inter-states Council under Art. 263, (ii) establishment of an Inter-states Trade and Commerce Commission, (iii) treating inter-states river waters as national assets and enacting legislation for dispute resolution, (iv) appointing only persons of eminence and detached outlook as Governors in consultation with concerned Chief Ministers and respecting their five year term, (v) using Art 365 only as a last resort after action under Art. 256, 257, 355 etc. fails, (vi) deciding questions of majority support only on the floor of the House, and (vii) in case of a 'hung house,' election of the Chief Minister by the House.

There are other institutional arrangements whereby the Union may exercise superintendence, direction and control over the states administration:

The head of the states Executive is the Governor who is appointed by the President. The governor acts not merely as the constitutional head of states but also as the agent of the Centre, as the eyes and ears of the Centre in the states. The Union Government may bring a states under the President rule (pseudonym for Centre) under Art. 356, if it is satisfied on its own or on receipt of a Report from the Governor of the states that the government of the states "cannot be carried on in accordance with the provisions of the Constitution." In such a situation, powers and functions of Government of the states are assumed by the Union Government. Art. 356 is the reserve power of the Centre to dismiss any states Government which is politically unacceptable to it, besides providing a way out where no political party or coalition of parties is able to command majority support in the Legislature.

There is a single integrated judicial system for the Union and the states which administer both the Union and the States' laws. The Supreme Court has 'original jurisdiction' in any dispute between the Government of India and any state/ states or between two or more states. Not only is there a separation between the executive and the judiciary, conditions have been created to ensure judicial independence. The judiciary has been given the power to declare a law to be unconstitutional if it is beyond the jurisdiction of the legislature according to the distribution of powers provided for by the Constitution or if it is in contravention of the fundamental rights or of any other mandatory provisions of the Constitution (Art. 13). The judiciary can thus look into matters respecting the jurisdiction of the legislature but not into the "wisdom" of legislative policy. The Supreme Court of India has held {*Synthetics and Chemicals Ltd Vs state of U.P.*, 1990} that the Court would interpret the intent of some legislation emerging out of the three Lists of legislative powers, and that this interpretation has to be such as to treat the Constitution as an organic document for the attainment of undisputed national goals. Earlier, a similar view about federalism was expressed by Justice Beg (in *state of Rajasthan Vs Union of India*, 1977)that the extent of federation (in India) is largely watered down by the needs of progress and development of a country which has to be nationally integrated, politically and economically coordinated, and socially, intellectually and spiritually uplifted. Much earlier, Justice Subha Rao had analysed the federal character of the Indian Constitution {*state of West Bengal Vs Union of India*, 1963}: "The Constitution distributes the sovereign powers between the coordinate constitutional entities, namely the Union and states. This concept implies that one cannot encroach upon the governmental functions of the other, unless the Constitution provides for such interference. This Court has the constitutional power and corrective duty to prevent encroachment, either overtly or covertly, by the Union on state field, or vice versa, and thus maintain the balance of power." This role of the Court as guarantor of the federal structure was asserted subsequently (*Golaknath* case, 1965) when the Indian Constitution was characterised as a federal constitution in which the judiciary was not only the protector of the constitution but also its sole interpreter and this position could not be changed by some ordinary legislation. Then, (in the *Bommai* case, 1994), the Supreme Court accepted federalism as a basic feature of the Constitution of India because "the federal principle is dominant in our Constitution in as much as the states are sovereign in the field which is left to them and they have an independent constitutional existence and they have an important role to play in the political, social, educational and cultural life of the people as the Union; the states are neither satellites nor agents of the Centre."

An important feature of India's Fiscal Federalism is revenue sharing between the Union and the states. Finally,

Parliament is empowered to make such grants as it deems necessary to providing financial assistance for any state in need. Such grants can be block grants or specific categorical grants. There is a clear vertical imbalance between (1) the powers of taxation assigned to the Union and the states and (2) the social and economic responsibilities assigned to the states. That is, the states' responsibilities exceed their own-source revenues.. But, the Finance Commission, the Planning Commission, and the National Development Council provide mechanisms for periodically correcting this imbalance and for allowing the states to better discharge their responsibilities. These forums cater to the grievances of the states, which they redress to the extent possible.

The Constitution provides that the distribution between the Union and the states of the net proceeds of taxes that are to be divided between them, and the allocation between states of the respective shares of such proceeds, shall be done on the recommendations of a Finance Commission that is appointed by the president every five years. The Commission also recommends the principles that should govern grants-in-aid to the states. The grants are both a means to assist development schemes in states lacking adequate financial resources and an instrument to exercise control and coordination over the states' welfare schemes.

An important feature of the financial relations between Union and states is the provision for revenue sharing between the Union and states. The following provisions of the Constitution are noteworthy in this connection.

(1) There are duties levied by the Union but collected and appropriated by the states, such as stamp duties and excise duties on medicine and toilet preparations.

(2) There are taxes levied and collected by the Union but assigned wholly to the states, for example, succession duties, estate duty, terminal taxes, taxes on railway fares and freights etc.

(3) There are taxes levied and collected by the Union and distributed between the Union and the states. This is the position of taxes on income other than agricultural income.

(4) There are taxes and duties which are levied and collected by the Union and may be distributed between the Union and the states if Parliament by law so provides. This is the position of excise duties other than duties on medicinal and toilet preparations.

Parliament is empowered to make such grants as it may deem necessary to give financial assistance to any state which is in need of such assistance. Such grants may either be block grants or specific grants.

It appears as if there is a clear vertical imbalance between (1) the powers of taxation assigned to the Union and the states and (2) the social and economic responsibilities assigned to the states. That is, the states' responsibilities exceed their own-source revenues. This arrangement is intended to permit each order of government to do what it is thought to do best; that is, it recognizes that the Centre is perhaps in the best position to collect certain kinds of taxes and to expend and redistribute tax revenues for equitable purposes nationwide, while states and their local governments are in the best position to manage developmental programs and to deliver most services because they are closest to the people.

Resource transfers authorized (under Art. 275) on the recommendations of the Finance Commission are known as statutory grants; those authorized (under Art. 282) on the recommendations of the Planning Commission are known as discretionary grants. When grants to the states are recommended by the Finance Commission — which is a statutory body — the Union government is constitutionally obligated to authorize the grants; hence the Union's authority with respect to grants does not add to its powers. But discretionary grants recommended by the Planning Commission — which is not a statutory body — are at the discretion of the Union government and thus political in nature. As such, they are criticized for causing the states' abject dependence on the Union — a dependence that is said to further enable the Union government to discriminate between states. Plan grants, provided for under Article 282, are 50-50 matching grants, which means that the Union government issues a grant equal to the sum that the state has raised through its own resources. It also means that states have to fall in line with Union policies, priorities, and preferences in issuing matching grants and also dovetail their own funds to Union allocations.

Because the Union grants are routed through central ministries to their counterparts in the states, each Union ministry is in a position to use the strings of financial power to superintend, direct, and control the corresponding state department. In this way, besides the territorial or horizontal federation set up by the Constitution, a sort of vertical federation has come into being. Various ministries of the government of India issue grants to corresponding ministries of state governments and, in this way, they are in a position to dictate and supervise departments of state governments. A vertical federation has resulted in which, through matching grants, the departments of Central and state governments on the same subject form a unit for the purposes of programmes and expenditure on the same. The state level bodies are merely implementing bodies and not the ones to consider the policies on the same level for the state as the Planning Commission does for the whole country.

There are both formal institutional and informal political arrangements for Centre-states coordination. Among the formal mechanisms are the Planning Commission, Finance Commission, National Development Council, Inter-state Council, National Integration Council, Zonal Councils, tribunals for adjudicating specific disputes, and various commissions and committees to look into specific aspects of Union-state relations. The informal mechanisms include ministerial and departmental meetings, conferences of constitutional functionaries and of political executives, and the governors' and chief ministers' conferences that are convened by the president and the prime minister. These informal arrangements are aimed at laying down procedural norms of conduct, particularly over such issues as the sharing of central taxes and the Union's intervention in states' affairs, and at evolving a common policy on such trans-governmental issues as the environment, communications, and health. Similarly, such informal mechanisms evolve conventions of governance on questions of states' rights, interstate trade and commerce, sharing of river waters, interstate communications, and other matters.

As per the recommendations of the Sarkaria Commission, the National Development Council (NDC) and the Zonal Councils were to supplement an Inter-Governmental Council (IGC). The NDC was to be known as the National Economic and Development Council (NEDC) and the IGC would perform functions as laid down in Art.263. Thus, both the two bodies, under the chairmanship of the Prime Minister, would be performing distinct functions—the NEDC dealing with matters of socio-economic planning and development, and the IGC the remaining functions in the inter-state relations. While the Zonal Councils were to act independently of the IGC, the latter was to be a standing consultative body to review parliamentary legislation affecting the states. However, the Zonal Councils were to provide the first level of discussions on inter-state issues, and the IGC would select matters of national importance and of common interest. The Sarkaria Commission had envisioned an advisory role for the IGC and yet had believed that the Council would build mutual trust and confidence, emerging as the major instrument for discussing policies affecting inter-governmental relations. This was an optimism that was not in consonance with existing political realities. The time has come to stop believing that only the NDC represents the interests of the whole nation in planning.

The First Five Year Plan had recommended that "in a country the size of India, where the states have under the Constitution full autonomy within their own sphere of duties, it is necessary to have a forum such as National Development Council (NDC) at which from time to time the Prime Minister of India and the Chief Ministers of states can review the working of the plan and of its various aspects." Consequently, the government established the NDC in 1952, and it is now composed of the Prime Minister, Chief Ministers of all the states, and members of the Planning Commission. The NDC is required to supervise the work of national planning, to recommend measures for the achievement of plan targets and to consider important questions of social and economic policy affecting national development. The state governments submit their five year plans to the Planning Commission which prepares the National Plan and, after its approval by the Central government, the NDC goes through it. The recommendations of the NDC are taken into consideration by the Planning Commission before the final shape is given. The process represents the principle of cooperative federalism. While its terms of reference originally expect the NDC to review the working of the National Plan from time to time, in practice the NDC makes recommendations pertaining to the overall size and structure of the Plan. Also, the NDC ensures a coordinated implementation of the Plan. Because of the coordinated- concerted approach of involving the Centre and the states, the NDC is able to ensure a balanced development in different regions of the country. The NDC is a policy-making body and its recommendations are not just advisory suggestions but policy-decisions and policy-directives. It is a national forum for planning which gives informal sanction to the underlying concept of cooperation between the Centre and the states. It brings states into an organic relationship with the organization of national planning. It occupies an important position in the Indian federal set up as it consists of the chief executives of the Central and state governments and, therefore, its advice can hardly be distinguished from a clear mandate.

The Indian Constitution would seem, in the end, to create a "cooperative union" of states rather than a dual polity What is being observed now is federal restructuring through politically developed rules and conventions, without disturbing the basic scheme of the Constitution. The actual working of cooperative federalism in India has entailed the Union's exercising its influence rather than its constitutional authority. Exigencies of coalition politics have forced the Union and state governments to share power. The Union has more often played the role of a facilitator in interstate disputes than that of an arbitrator. A redistribution of powers — through decentralisation and the devolution of authority from the Union to the states and from the states to the panchayats and municipalities — is serving to facilitate the attainment of the objectives of the Constitution: unity, social justice, and democracy. A healthy sign is the growing realisation that inter-governmental relations need to focus more on the needs of the citizens——particularly in welfare policy areas—rather than on questions of turf and jurisdiction. The debate is today less about division of powers and more about recognition of roles and responsibilities. Federal governance is a mechanism that is suitable to countries like India where there are different levels of development and different levels of resources available. For that, some power sharing is required in the system of governance. For that sense of accommodation to be there, a paradigm shift is needed in which democracy need not be just representative but a participatory democracy.

Further Readings

Balakrishnan, Rajiv, *Jharkhand Matters*, (Konark: Delhi: 2004).

Chatterjee, Partha, *State and Politics in India*, (Oxford: Delhi, 1997).

Chopra, Pran, *The Supreme Court versus the Constitution: A Challenge to Federalism*, (New Delhi: Sage, 2006).

deSouza, Peter Ronald, *India's Political Parties*, (New Delhi: Sage, 2006).

Hasan, Zoya, *Quest for Power: Oppositional Movements and Post-Congress Politics in Uttar Pradesh*, (New Delhi: Oxford, 1998).

Jayal, Niraja Gopal, *Democarcy in India*, (New Delhi: Oxford, 2001)

Kashyap, Subhash C. and Gert W. Kueck, *Reviewing the Constitution*, (Delhi: Shipra, 2000).

Kashyap, Subhash C., *Constitutional Reforms: Problems, Prospects and Prospectives*, (New Delhi: Radha, 2004).

Kirpal, B.N., Rajeev Dhavan (et.al.), *Supreme But Not Infallible*, (New Delhi: Oxford, 2000).

Noorani, A.G., *Constitutional Questions in India: The President,*

Parliament and the states, (New Delhi: Oxford, 2000).

Panandiker, V.A. Pai, *Fifty Years of Swaraj: Highlights and Shadows,* (Delhi: Konark, 2008).

Prakash, Amit, *Jharkhand: Politics of Development and Identity,* (New Delhi: Orient Longman, 2001).

Pylee, M.V., *Our Constitution, Government and Politics,* (Delhi: Universal, 2002).

Roy, Ramashray, *Democracy in India: Forms and Substance,* (New Delhi: Shipra, 2005).

Rudolph, Lloyd and Susanne Hoeber Rudolph, *Explaining Indian Democarcy: The Realm of Ideas,* (New Delhi: Oxford: 2008).

Vashum, R., *Nagas' Right to Self-Determination,* (New Delhi: Mittal, 2000).

Vora, Rajendra and Suhas Palshikar, *Indian Democarcy: Meanings and Practices,* (New Delhi: Sage, 2004).

5

Some Unanswered issues of Indian Federalism

In the Constitution of India, there are certain avenues of potential federal conflicts that include working of several constitutional provisions about the separation of powers between different branches and tiers of government. 'Emergency,' roles of the President and the Governor, competence over certain areas of governance, fiscal federalism, etc are some of these areas.. In spite of being contrary to the Constitutional provisions, different attacks on the federal structure are not being given proper academic attention. Areas that need analysis include Executive Orders from the Union to the states, Union's "fact-finding" teams to the states, Union and the problem of Law-and-Order in the states, Subordinate Legislation and question of Autonomy of states. All this becomes relevant in the light of what is being propagated

A constitutional governance in a large federation is possible only if the autonomy of each organ of the government is respected and the delicate balance of power is maintained, not only among the different tiers of government, but also between the executive, legislature and the judiciary. Over the years, there has been a shift in this balance from both the executive and the legislature to the judiciary. Such a shift might be welcomed by those who believe that the legislature has lost its right to manage its own proceedings, as provided in the Constitution. The plea has been given that it is the partisan speakers and governors who have subverted constitutional governance, and that the executive has failed to provide a 'good governance,' thus making a 'judicial activism' imperative. It was a judgement of far-reaching consequences when the Court identified the Right to Life with a right to "good / quality life," and the subsequent measures have definitely added to the quality-content in the life of the citizens. But saying that every citizen has a right to get good quality drinking water is one thing; and it would be a different matter if the courts were to decide the modalities and the time frame and the budget for doing that and then to monitor the progress of implementation. Directing the executive and the legislature to perform their statutory obligations is one thing but it would be over-burdening the already over-burdened courts if they were to decide questions such as the timings of entry of heavy-traffic in the cities.

The majority judgement of the Supreme Court in the Bommai case of 1993 had claimed the power to review the imposition of the President's Rule in the states. What the Constitution expects of the Courts is not to interfere in the discretionary powers of the President and the Governors, in matters of appointment of the Prime Minister or the Chief Minister, unless such an exercise of power was *mala fide*. The framers of the Constitution had not visualized the day when the Court would not only order the legislature to conduct a vote of confidence but would also lay down in detail how the proceedings of the legislature should be conducted in this regard (e.g., Uttar Pradesh, in 1998, and Jharkhand, in 2005). Further, the Supreme Court can be approached by an individual directly only in case of breaches of Fundamental Rights; and none of the framers of the Constitution had ever asserted that the fundamental rights include a right to be appointed as Chief Minister. Executive and legislative functions of governance cannot be judicially managed and the authority of the Constitution should not be questioned. Yet, there is a clear shift.

The argument in favour of a shift has been advanced that there has been public support for judicial interference because of defaults of governments and legislatures. A sensation-loving Press has manipulated the public opinion to applaud the intrusive roles in areas that were constitutionally reserved for different branches of government. How the situation has changed, over the last four decades, is clear from two extreme examples: In 1964, the state legislative assembly of Uttar Pradesh had ordered that two judges of the state High Court be produced before it for contempt of the House; and at the time, the Supreme Court (via an 'advisory opinion') had held that the High Court / Supreme Court have the power to decide constitutionality of legislation but cannot interfere with the legislative proceedings. But, in 2005, the Supreme Court decided that its own order was to be taken as notice for the session of the State's Assembly and ordered that the proceedings of the House be video-recorded and produced before the Court for review, and deciding by itself the order of the business-proceedings of the House. What has been overlooked is the dictum that any good governance in a federation is possible only if every branch and tier of government exhibits a commitment to constitutional norms.

No doubt, Articles 122 and 212 of the Constitution prohibit the court from making any enquiry of proceedings of Parliament or state legislature on the grounds of irregularity of procedure. The courts are prohibited, under these Articles, from making any enquiry against officers or members of Parliament who exercise powers under the Constitution. The Supreme Court has maintained that the courts do have the power to enquire if the procedure in the House is illegal. As long as officers and members of Parliament exercise powers in accordance with the provisions of the Constitution, the courts will not interfere. By corollary, if the Speaker exceeds or transgresses the powers vested in him, or fails to take appropriate action, the courts would be within their constitutional limits to intervene and direct. However, there can be no interference in the day to day functioning of the legislature. Some doubts were expressed as to whether a 'Pro-term' Speaker has the authority to conduct confidence-vote proceedings. Article 212 (2) of the Constitution stipulates that "no office or member of the legislature of a state in whom powers are vested by or under this Constitution for regulating procedure or the conduct of business, or for maintaining order in the legislature, shall be subject to the jurisdiction of any court in respect of the exercise by him of those powers." Clearly, in the application of this Article, there is to be no distinction between an elected Speaker or a pro-term Speaker. Article 180 (2) says that, in the absence of the Speaker and the Deputy Speaker, " such person as may be determined by the rules of the procedure of the Assembly, or, if no such person is present, such other person as may be determined by the Assembly, shall act as Speaker." A pro-term Speaker enjoys all the powers of a regular Speaker.

In spite of the balance of emphasis now getting shifted, the Constitutional requirements are clear and cannot be overlooked: Other than matters concerning impeachment, the legislatures cannot discuss the conduct of judges of High

Court or Supreme Court (Art. 121 & 211); there is immunity from court proceedings for the President and the Governors (Art. 361); the courts cannot look into the validity of proceedings of the legislatures (Art. 122 & 212).

Article 256 of the Constitution lays down that " the executive power of every state shall be exercised as to ensure compliance with the laws made by Parliament and any existing laws which apply in that state and the executive power of the Union shall extend to giving of such directions to a state as may appear to the Government of India to be necessary for that purpose." However, the Supreme Court, in the *state of Rajasthan Vs Union of India*, held in 1979 that this does not empower the Union to interfere in any matter pertaining to the exclusive concern of a state and if the Prime Minister issues any directive to a state in the exclusive state sphere, such directive shall not be binding upon the state. However, Art. 257(1) elaborates that "the executive power of the Union shall extend to the giving of such directions to a state as may appear to the Government of India to be necessary for that purpose." It is rather obvious that, under this provision, the Union can issue a direction only where some action of a state government is likely to prejudice the exercise of the executive power of the Union" *[J Fazle Ali* in the *state of Rajasthan Vs Union of India, SC 1977].*In cases of matters falling within state jurisdiction, like the maintenance of law and order, Art. 257(1) cannot be applied.

It is constitutionally natural that the Union government should have the power to ensure that the state governance is done as required by the Constitution, and that the union has the power to suppress violence in a state so that the Constitution can function as it was intended to function. As Seervai says, "a power essential for the existence of federal government cannot be said to impair the federal principle....Internal disturbance in a state would prevent the union from executing the powers entrusted to it and interfere with its property and services in the states, so that the Union could deal with such disturbances on its own....Just as in the case of a conflict between a valid state law and a valid Union law, the Union law prevails, so also a question may arise as to the conflict between the valid exercise of executive power by the Union and the states and, equally logically, Art 257 provides that the executive power of every state shall be so exercised as not to impede or prejudice the exercise of the executive power of the Union. To make this general declaration effective, Art.257 provides that the executive power of the Union shall extend to giving such directions to a state as may appear to the Government of India to be necessary for that purpose" (1)

The power of the Union government to give directions to the state governments is fortified by provisions of Art. 365. If a state government flouts the directions given by the Union government, under Art. 257, the President can well take a view that the situation has arisen in which it is not possible to run the government of a state in accordance with the provisions of the Constitution. Such a sanction is necessary to prevent flouting of directions of the Union government. Such a provision should not be seen as contrary to the federal principle. For the working of a federal constitution, the Union executive has to have the power of giving directions to the state executive as the executive authority of the federation extends to states also.

When the Union government, in the exercise of its executive power to a state government, under Articles 256-7 of the Constitution, issues any directions, it becomes the duty of the governor to keep the union government informed as to how such directions are being implemented by the state government. It would be erroneous to assume that the Governor is subordinate or a subservient agent of the Union government because he is holder of an independent constitutional office. However, as far as specified functions are concerned where the Constitution requires him to perform as agent of the Union, the Governor is accountable to the President. In this context, Article 159 is also relevant which specifies the oath of office of the Governor binding him to preserve, protect and defend the Constitution and the law. As a link between the Union and the state, it is the duty of the Governor to keep the Union of the affairs of the state administration whenever he feels that matters are not going on in accordance with the Constitution. The Governor, thus, assists the Union in discharging its responsibilities towards the state. He becomes an agent of the Union in certain special circumstances, e.g., when a proclamation under Art. 356 is in operation.

Article 167 of the Constitution entitles the Governor to have full information of the decisions of the state government and of developments in the state. Since he can seek all information from the Government, it is obvious that nothing is to be kept away from the knowledge of the Governor and everything has to be communicated to him. The Governor has to keep himself abreast of the happenings in the state so that he may be an effective constitutional-head. Through his fortnightly reports, the Governor keeps the Union government adequately informed of the events and developments in the state and the manner in which the government of the state was being carried on. They have to keep themselves informed about key sectors of administration in the state so that their reports could provide the Union with meaningful information and, at the same time, give timely advice and warning, if necessary, to the Chief Minister also. In making these reports, the Governor has to act according to his own judgement. The

Sarkaria Commission on Centre-state Relations had recommended that, while sending such reports, the Governor should normally take his Chief Minister into confidence, unless there are over-riding reasons to the contrary.

Under the Constitution, the Union is neither a guardian of the states nor, in a federal system, can it act as their supervisor. A forced resignation, or dismissal, of a Governor is only an exercise of unconstitutional pressure on other Governors. Seervai observes[2] that, if in the honest discharge of his functions, the Governor adopts a line not in conformity with the Union government, then the latter would not be justified in advising the removal of the Governor; otherwise it would mean that the union executive would effectively control the state executive which is opposed to the basic structure of our Constitution. The Committee of Governors, appointed by the President, in its Report (1971) had asserted that functions of the governors were laid down in the Constitution and, therefore, he was in no sense an agent of the President; and that there is no power vested in any authority to issue any directions to the Governor or lay down any code or rules for his guidance.

As per Art. 164 (1) & (2), the Chief Minister of a state is to be appointed by the Governor. Naturally, in conformity with the spirit of the Constitution (and according to Art 164-ii), the council of ministers, headed by the chief minister, shall be collectively responsible to the Assembly. A governor has the authority under Article 163 to exercise any of his functions 'in his discretion.' And where the governor acts in his own discretion, no juridical review is possible. (*Pratap Singh Rane v Government of Goa, AIR 1999 Bom 53, 91, paragraphs 29, 36 (DB)* as cited by P/M Bakshi in The Constitution of India, Universal Law Publishing Co, 2000, page 148.) In *Hargovind Pant v Raghukul Tilak (AIR 1979*

SC 1109), the Supreme Court held that the office of the governor is not an employment under the Government of India; he is not subordinate or subservient or under control of the Government of India, nor is he amenable to its directions; nor is he accountable to it for the manner in which he carries out his functions and duties. According to the court, the governor's 'is an independent constitutional office which is not subject to the control of the Government of India.' The Guwahati High court had ruled that the governor is the 'sole and exclusive authority' to appoint the chief minister. In *Jogendranath v Assam* (*AIR 1982 Gau 25*) the court held that the Governor as the head of the state 'is the sole judge to ascertain as to who commanded the support of the majority in the assembly.

It has to be at the discretion of the Governor to decide as to who, among the leaders of various parties / coalitions, would be in a position to command a majority on the floor of the House. The deciding factor has to be, not the size of a party, but the ability of an individual to carry the House with him. In a situation where no single party enjoys an absolute majority, it cannot be binding on the Governor to invite the leader of the single-largest party to try forming the government. Such a leader cannot claim an absolute right to be invited to 'try to form' a government; and the largest party may not be ultimately in a position to obtain the support of other members in the House. The Governor may feel that the leader of a party with not that much of numerical strength in the House may be in a position to obtain support of other parties, and in such a case the Governor has to act as per his discretion. Even the Sarkaria Commission on Centre-state relations had left an ultimate option for the discretion of the Governor, while recommending an order of sounding out parties where no single party gets a majority: first, a pre-poll alliance claiming majority support, then the largest single party seeking a claim, then a post-election coalition with all parties in government, and fourth a post-election alliance with some parties in government and others providing outside support; and after going through this process he "should select a leader who in his judgement is most likely to command a majority in the Assembly." Ultimately, it is the Governor who has to decide who that leader might be.

The governor holds office for a term of five years, during the pleasure of the President and, of course, he can resign from the office at anytime. First of all, 'pleasure of the President' does not confer any sanction for an arbitrary behaviour. Secondly, no constitutional or civil functionary can be removed from his office without having an opportunity to explain his actions and conduct. This provision would cover the recall of a Governor because recall is an adverse action and an opportunity to explain the conduct ought to be afforded to the Governor also before an adverse action is actually taken. If the Union government is of the view, at any time that a governor is not discharging his constitutional duties, an explanation may be sought and only if the explanation is not satisfactory an adverse action be taken. In this context, the Sarkaria Commission had recommended : " save when the President is satisfied that, in the interest of the security of the state, it is not expedient to do so, as a mater of healthy practice, whenever it is proposed to terminate the tenure of a Governor before the expiry of the normal term of five years, he should be informally appraised of the grounds of the proposed action and afforded a reasonable opportunity for showing cause against it... Any other inference would render clause (3) of Art. 156 largely otiose... It is desirable that the President should get the explanation, if any, submitted by the Governor against his proposed removal from office, examined by an advisory group consisting of the Vice President of India and the Speaker of the House of the People and a retired Chief Justice of India. After receiving the recommendations of this group, the President may pass such orders in the case as he may deem fit."[3] Pleasure has to be rational exercise, consistent with the dignity of constitutional authority. In his address to state Governors, President Zail Singh had said, on 9 April 1983, that "in our Constitution, there is no power vested in any authority to issue any directions to the Governor or lay down any code of rules for his guidance."[4] In the same spirit, the Supreme Court had held, in 1979: " It is not material that a Governor holds office during the pleasure of the President. It is a constitutional provision for determination of the term of office of the Governor and it does not make the Government of India an employer of the Governor....This office is not subordinate or subservient to the Government of India. He is not amenable to the discretion of the government of India nor is he accountable to them for the manner in which he carries out his functions and duties. He is an independent constitutional office which is not subject to the control of the Government of India."[5]

'Public Order' is clearly a concern of the states (entry 1 of state List) and it is for this reason that Art. 352 (empowering imposition of 'Emergency') uses the words 'internal disturbance' as a cause for such imposition. Internal Disturbance is explained by the Report of the (Sarkaria) Commission on Centre-state Relations [Vol. 1, p. 168] in the sense of 'domestic chaos' taking the colour of a security threat and leading to a breakdown of the constitutional machinery of the state. It is to be noted that the 44th Amendment to the Constitution, in 1978, deleted Art. 257(1) which had read: "The Government of India may deploy an armed force of the union or any other armed force subject to the control of the union for dealing with any grave situation of law and order in any state." It is significant that the words 'grave situation of law and order' (Art. 257A) were deleted but the words 'internal disturbance' in Art 355 were retained and then substituted with words 'armed rebellion.' Now the position is that maintenance of public order remains the exclusive responsibility of the state government unless the threats to public order are so grave and consistent as to amount to 'internal disturbance,' 'domestic chaos,' or 'armed rebellion.' Any isolated incident or aberration cannot warrant the description 'breakdown of constitutional machinery.'A deterioration in law-and-order cannot constitutionally justify imposition of President's Rule in some state. There have been cases of severe breakdown of law and order in states that were governed by the same political party that governed at the Centre. It is yet another matter that, for political expediency, such threats are given to non- friendly state governments, on the plea of deteriorating law and order situation. Similarly, the plea of mal-administration, or financial mis-management, on the part of a state government, if such government continues to enjoy the support of the majority in the state legislature, cannot properly justify Union interference. In the federal polity of India, the Constitution had not made the Union a monitor on matters placed under state jurisdiction. Sending Teams of Union ministers / officials to the states to obtain desired reports was never visualised by the Constitution. It amounts to unconstitutional intimidation of states ruled by governments of parties other than those at the Centre.

The Parliamentary procedures, in India, prohibit asking questions, placing adjournment or other motions if the subject matter is not of concern of the government of India (such as law and order in a state). What is prohibited to the Parliament cannot be assumed by the Union executive.

A deterioration in law-and-order cannot constitutionally justify imposition of President's Rule in some state. There have been cases of severe breakdown of law and order in states that were governed by the same political party that governed at the Centre. It is yet another matter that, for political expediency, such threats are given to non-friendly state governments, on the plea of deteriorating law and order situation. Similarly, the plea of mal-administration, or financial mis-management, on the part of a state government, if such government continues to enjoy the support of the majority in the state legislature, cannot properly justify Union interference. In the federal polity of India, the Constitution had not made the Union a monitor on matters placed under state jurisdiction. Sending teams of Union ministers / officials to the states to obtain desired reports was never visualised by the Constitution.

Maintenance of public order is exclusively a state subject till the law and order situation deteriorates to the extent where aid of central armed forces becomes necessary. The crucial point here is that such central forces are to aid the state government, not to supplant or replace it. No doubt, under Art 355 and under Entry 2A of List I, the Union government can send such forces on its own, without any request coming from the state government, and even against the wishes of the state government. Still, such deployment would be to aid the state government overcome problems of public order. In these situations, the Union government cannot assume the sole responsibility for dealing with an internal disturbance by superseding or excluding the state police and other authorities responsible for maintaining public order. As pointed by the Sarkaria Commission, the Union government "cannot deploy, in contravention of the wishes of a state government, its armed forces to deal with a relatively less serious public order problem which is unlikely to escalate" and which the government of the state might be in a position to take care of on its own.

The Constitution (Art. 257) provides that "the executive power of the Union shall extend to giving such directions to a state as may appear to the Government of India to be necessary for that purpose." Since, under the Constitution, the Union has the power to give directions to the states, there has to be some provision to take sanctions against non-compliance with the directions.

Article 355 of the Constitution covers steps necessary to ensure that the government of every state is carried on in accordance with the provisions of the Constitution and it is with this end in view that the Constitution has conferred upon the Union the power under Art. 356. Even in the Constituent Assembly, it was felt that it is the duty of the Union government to protect the states against external aggression, internal disturbance and domestic chaos and to see that the Constitution is worked in a proper manner both in the states and the Union and that if the responsible government, as contemplated by the Constitution functions properly, the Union will not interfere. Once the duty of the state has been enumerated, under Art.355, to function in accordance with the Constitution, remedial measures are elaborated, under Art 356, when the government of a state cannot be carried out in accordance with the Constitution. Art. 356 provided for a report about the constitutional functioning of the state government from the state Governor to the President. Even without the report of the Governor, the President can obtain such information 'otherwise,' from other sources. These two articles imply that, for the proper discharge of its responsibilities, the Union has a right to expect and the Governor a duty to send reports on important developments in the state that appear to the Governor to leading towards potential or actual situation of external aggression or internal disturbance or failure of the constitutional machinery in the state. After such an information has reached, the President may by proclamation (a) assume to himself the executive powers of the state, and (b) declare that the powers of the state legislature shall be exercised by or under the authority of Parliament. The Governor's report falls within the ambit of his discretionary powers [Art. 163-ii].

Constitutional breakdown occurs when a government resigns following its defeat in the legislature and no alternative ministry, enjoying the support of the legislature, can be formed; when even a coalition government is not possible when the majority party refuses to form a government; when the state government fails to carry out the directions of the Union government; when the state executive flouts the judgement of the Court that may have declared a state law as unconstitutional; when the state executive does not obey the directions of the state legislature; when normal legislative procedure is paralysed by the members or otherwise; when the state government has no control over the administrative and civil service of the state; and when the state government seeks to use its constitutional powers for purposes not authorised by the Constitution and does not heed to warnings or other corrective measures. One such situation under 'constitutional breakdown' is elaborated in Art. 365 : " Where any state has failed to comply with, or to give effect to, any directions given in exercise of the executive power of the Union under any provisions of this Constitution, it shall be lawful for the President to hold that a situation has arisen in which the Government of the state cannot be carried on in accordance with the provisions of this Constitution." However, in the light of the Supreme Court judgement in the Bommai case(3 SCC, 1994), it is clear that the directions given by the Union executive should be lawful and that state's failure to comply with them should lead to a situation where governance according to Constitution (Art. 356-I) was not possible.

Besides many other situations, two specific situations were pointed out by the Sarkaria Commission in which it would be improper to invoke Art. 356: (a) in situations of internal subversion, physical breakdown or non-compliance with the constitutional directions of the union government, when the President gives no prior warning or opportunity to the state government to correct itself; and (b) when in response to the prior warning or notice or to an informal or formal direction under Articles 256, 257 etc, the state government either applies the corrective and thus complies with the direction, or satisfies the Union executive that the warning or direction was based on incorrect facts.

Maintenance of public order is exclusively a state subject till the law and order situation deteriorates to the extent where aid of central armed forces becomes necessary. The crucial point here is that such central forces are to aid the state government, not to supplant or replace it. No doubt, under Art 355 and under Entry 2A of List I, the Union government can send such forces on its own, without any request coming from the state government, and even against the wishes of the state government. Still, such deployment would be to aid the state government overcome problems of public order. In these situations, the Union government cannot assume the sole responsibility for dealing with an internal disturbance by superseding or excluding the state police and other authorities responsible for maintaining public order. As pointed out by the Sarkaria Commission, the Union government "cannot deploy, in contravention of the wishes of a state government, its armed forces to deal with a relatively less serious public order problem which is unlikely to escalate" and which the government of the state might be in a position to take care of on its own.

Article 355 of the Constitution covers steps necessary to ensure that the government of every state is carried on in accordance with the provisions of the Constitution and it is with this end in view that the Constitution has conferred upon the Union the power under Art. 356. Even in the Constituent Assembly, it was felt that it is the duty of the Union government to protect the states against external aggression, internal disturbance and domestic chaos and to see that the Constitution is worked in a proper manner both in the states and the Union and that if the responsible government, as contemplated by the Constitution functions properly, the Union will not interfere.

Once the duty of the state has been enumerated, under Art.355, to function in accordance with the Constitution, remedial measures are elaborated, under Art 356, when the government of a state cannot be carried out in accordance with the Constitution. Art. 356 provided for a report about the constitutional functioning of the state government from the state Governor to the President. Even without the report of the Governor, the President can obtain such information 'otherwise,' from other sources. These two articles imply that, for the proper discharge of its responsibilities, the Union has a right to expect, and the Governor a duty to send, reports on important developments in the state that appear to the Governor to leading towards potential or actual situation of external aggression or internal disturbance or failure of the constitutional machinery in the state. After such an information has reached, the President may by proclamation (a) assume to himself the executive powers of the state, and (b) declare that the powers of the state legislature shall be exercised by or under the authority of Parliament. The Governor's report falls within the ambit of his discretionary powers [Art. 163-ii].

One situation under 'constitutional breakdown' is elaborated in Art. 365 : " Where any state has failed to comply with, or to give effect to, any directions given in exercise of the executive power of the Union under any provisions of this Constitution, it shall be lawful for the President to hold that a situation has arisen in which the Government of the state cannot be carried on in accordance with the provisions of this Constitution." However, in the light of the Supreme Court judgement in the Bommai case (3 SCC, 1994), it is clear that the directions given by the Union executive should be lawful and that state's failure to comply with them should lead to a situation where governance according to Constitution (Art. 356-I) was not possible.

Besides many other situations, two specific situations were pointed out by the Sarkaria Commission in which it would be improper to invoke Art. 356 : (a) in situations of internal subversion, physical breakdown or non-compliance with the constitutional directions of the union government, when the President gives no prior warning or opportunity to the state government to correct itself; and (b) when in response to the prior warning or notice or to an informal or formal direction under Articles 256, 257 etc., the state government either applies the corrective and thus complies with the direction, or satisfies the Union executive that the warning or direction was based on incorrect facts.

If one carefully analyses the constitutional provision "... a situation has arisen in which the government of a state cannot be carried on in accordance with the provisions of this Constitution...," then the operative word appears to be cannot. This implies impossibility of governance, not any difficulty in governance. It is clear that a Presidential proclamation, under Art. 356, should not be made upon a consideration which is extraneous to the purpose for which the power under Art. 356 is conferred, that is a breakdown of constitutional machinery in a state. It is clear that its use is to be made in cases of emergency: the very fact that the provisions in Art. 356 are included in Part XVIII as an 'emergency provision'—even though as the Supreme Court has said (in *State of Rajasthan Vs Union of India, 1977)*, it has no relation to an emergency of the kind dealt with in Art. 352—would lead to conclusion that the situation contemplated in Art 356 is not one of mere irregularity or difficulty, but one in the nature of an emergency—-a breakdown of constitutional machinery which calls for abnormal remedy. The cause for use of Art 356 cannot be for achieving 'good governance' in a state. It has to be a failure of the constitutional machinery.

In 1977, in the *State of Rajasthan Vs Union of India* [3SCC 592], the Supreme Court acknowledged that the Union government was competent to dissolve a state assembly under Art. 356 though, it was maintained, that the Court could examine whether the President issued the Proclamation on *malafide* or irrelevant considerations, as the satisfaction of the President is a subjective matter and cannot be put to objective tests: "The Supreme Court cannot interdict the use of powers under Art. 356 (i) unless and until resort to the provision, in a particular situation, is shown to be so grossly perverse and unreasonable as to constitute patent misuse of this provision or an excess of power on admitted facts. The most that one could say is that a dissolution against the wishes of the majority in a state assembly is a grave and serious matter. Perhaps it could be observed that it should be resorted to under Art 356(i) of the Constitution only when a 'critical situation' has arisen." Justice Bhagwati had observed, in this case: It {satisfaction of the President) would be a political judgement based on assessment of diverse and varied factors, fast changing situations, potential consequences, public reaction, motivations and response of different classes of people and their anticipated future behaviour and a host of other considerations. It cannot, therefore, by its very nature, be a fit subject-matter for judicial determinism and hence it is left to the subjective satisfaction of the Central government which is best in a position to decide it.

The Supreme Court had done an exhaustive analysis of Art. 356 in *S.R. Bommai Vs Union of India* (1994, 3SCC.1): The satisfaction of the President is to be formed on relevant material... Art. 74(2) merely bars an inquiry into the question whether any, and if so what, advice was rendered by the ministers to the President, and it does not bar the Court from calling upon the Council of Ministers (Union of India) to disclose to the Court the material upon which the President had formed the requisite satisfaction, as the material on the basis of which advice was tendered does not become part of the advice... The Proclamation under Art. 356(i) is not immune from judicial review and the Supreme/ High Court can strike down the Proclamation if it is found to be *malafide* or based on wholly irrelevant or extraneous grounds. In this case, the Supreme Court had sought to contain the Union urge to ride rough-shed over the states with the threat of dismissal under Art. 356. The intention of the Court appeared to be asking the Union government to first explore a solution other than imposition of the President's rule. In this light, one solitary departure from one or the other Article of the Constitution, on the part of the state government, cannot be reason enough for such imposition. The situation, in its totality, should have become such that the governance of the state could not be carried on in accordance with the constitution, in the absence of the President's rule.

Dr Ambedkar had discussed, in the Constituent Assembly, the remote possibility of Art. 356 being used and had hoped that the President would first take some alternate steps: "I hope the President will take proper precautions before actually suspending the administration of the provinces. I hope the first thing he will do would be to issue a mere warning to a province that has erred, that things were not happening in the way they were intended to happen in the Constitution. If that warning fails, the second thing for him will be to order an election allowing the people of he province to settle matters themselves. It is only when these two remedies fail that he would resort to this article."[6]

The Union governments, on occasions, have worked around the legal niceties and loopholes in circumventing limitations in the use of Art. 356. In 1977, when nine state governments were dismissed (though there was no constitutional breakdown), the absence of Rajya Sabha support was circumvented when the Union government held mid-term polls in these states before the deadline (of three months) of getting the Proclamation approved by both the houses of Parliament.

On the potential use of Art. 356, Sir Alladi Krishnaswamy Aiyar had observed in the Constituent Assembly, on 3 August 1949, that "it is only when there is a failure or breakdown of the constitutional machinery that the Union government will interfere." Though the intent of the framers of the Constitution was that the Art. 356 was to be used only when the whole machinery of government was broken down, in practice the Article has been used as a weapon of first resort. Whereas in the

Constituent Assembly, platitudes were expressed that provisions under Art 356 would never be called into operation and that they would remain a dead letter, in actual practice these provisions have been invoked over a hundred times. One wonders how the excessive use to this extent can justify its inclusion under the provisions dealing with "emergency."

NOTES

1. H.M. Seervai, *Constitutional Law of India*, Tripathi Bombay 1984, p. 1725.
2. *Ibid.*
3. Sarkaria Commission Report, 4:12 June, 1988.
4. *The Indian Express*, April 25, 1983.
5. *Hargovind Pant v. Dr Raghukul Tilak*, AIR *1978, SC 709.*
6. *Constituent Assembly Debates*, V. IX, pp. 176-7.

6

Distribution of Competencies in the Indian Federation

The essence of federalism is the existence of independent political decision-making at different levels of government. Yet, such decision-making cannot operate in isolation and inter-dependence in governance necessitates shared-governance. The philosophical foundation of the US federalism stipulated that a government is best if it governs the least and, therefore, only limited functions were given to the Union. This option did not exist in India because already there was a long historical tradition of centralisation of power and authority. Our philosophical foundation was that a government is best when it is able to bring about social transformation. Hence, the framers of the Constitution and the subsequent law-makers consciously ensured that the overwhelming majority of powers and authority was kept with the Union. In the process, we overlooked a philosophical foundation of our independence struggle: good governance is no substitute for self-governance. We discarded the federal principle that even if a function is not done best by a regional government, that power should not be assumed by the Union. This was not only against an accepted federal norm but also against the democratic principle of self-rule. The sharing of powers between Union and states came to a situation in which the Union had what powers it had but shared in the powers that the states had.

The constitutional division of responsibilities between the Centre and the states/ provinces is the basis of a federal structure. Responsibilities of various tiers of government are determined by the functions that are assigned to them. The ability and competence to perform these functions depend on the earmarking of sources of finance. Three factors contributed to an intensification of inter-governmental interaction during the twentieth century: the general trend to increased activity of governments at all levels creating more overlaps, the development of new policy areas such as the environment and energy not contemplated at the time the older federations were designed, and the changing conditions affecting over time the allocations of taxing powers and expenditure responsibilities to different governments and creating vertical and horizontal imbalances. These required intergovernmental transfers and processes and institutions for the periodic adjustment of financial relations among governments. Now as federations move into the twenty-first century, the interdependence inherent within all federal systems is being further extended and complicated by its widened scope increasingly embracing the international and municipal spheres as well.

The spirit of the Constitution of India was not on exclusiveness but on shared coordination. What has evolved is as if Union's powers are exclusive powers and States' powers are shared powers. This is creating serious problems for working of a federal system and it need to be studied and taken care of. The Constitution of India is a mechanism for sharing power in our social-pluralism that is territorially identified. The Constitution had envisaged a balance between the need for an effective Union/ Centre and effectively — empowered states. The federal system that emerged became the sound framework for the working of our Constitution. In spite of problems of balance-maintenance, the system has survived, though many of its federal features got eroded. In spite of great odds and great complexity, India as a nation has survived, because it is united as a Nation with the voluntary and natural agreement of its constituent units. Largely, this is due to the fact that the Constitution has worked as a functioning mechanism not just for resolving inter-governmental disputes but in maintaining a constitutional balance between the tiers of government.

The question of distribution of responsibilities and assignment of resources is linked to political culture also. It is not as if it is only now that we have started thinking whether this distribution is generally compatible with our society, political culture and economy. These concerns were before the makers of the Constitution also. It was definitely a concern that India, with so many of regional diversities, needed a centralised planning. It was a concern that some planned development was needed to remove regional disparities. Maintenance of unity and national integration was a major concern. The question is whether federalism was more compatible with the Indian society of 1947 or is it more relevant for our society at the beginning of the 21st Century. There is a widely-held scholarly belief that our society has largely remained stagnant. One perceptible change that has emerged is the emergence of the erstwhile non-participant actors, such as Dalits, the Backwards and some marginalised sections of minorities. The federalisation of the party system has altered the basic premises of inter-governmental relations, and has created new mechanisms that are impacting on the federal structure. It has led to the development of new ways of organising inter-state and the Union-state relations. Most of these newly-evolved structures are informal, even ad hoc, even 'para-constitutional.' All this has affected not only party politics and legislative configuration, but also the nature of political coalitions and alliances, inter-governmental relations and, consequently, the nature of distribution of responsibilities among governments at different levels.

Any discussion about distribution of powers and responsibilities would encompass the constitutional mechanisms that have been used for that end. It appears as if the constitutional discourse is about 'selection' of powers and not about the 'description' of powers that are to be distributed. Thus, existing provisions regarding our federal structure need to be particularly examined from the evolving perspectives of autonomy and integration. We have to balance the factors promoting federal-institutional model of self-rule with shared rule. The inherent notion of power-distribution and power-sharing arrangements is a question between the National and Regional constituents of our federation. This relationship between the sub-structures of Union and states is to be examined from the notion of competence — division and sharing of a subject. Areas of potential federal conflicts, that invite attention, include working of several constitutional provisions about Union's intervention in spheres of States' activities, distribution of financial resources, and other issues of fiscal federalism. It would not be sufficient, or appropriate, to assert that there is too much of centralisation because it is not the same level of centralisation or decentralisation in all subjects.

There are structural changes that have been introduced in the Indian federal system. This is an emergence of a sub-state structure and an evolution of multi-level federalism. This third tier is not functioning in isolation but is interacting with a range and variety of non-government institutions and voluntary-sector institutions. This interface has had an effect not only on a third tier but also on the other two, in a federal system. Any debate on a distribution of responsibility and of resources would remain incomplete if a constitutional position of the federal structure remains blurred, even after half a century of constitution working. Are the local bodies—the third tier—'institutions of self-government' (Article 243 G) or are they 'units of self-government' (Article 40)? Under which term are they merely an implementing agency of the Union and state projects, and under which terms do they acquire some autonomous status to discharge their responsibilities with commensurate resources to do the same? When funds are not allotted, and funds and functionaries are not given, and any independent status is merely on paper, then any conceptual, theoretical or action-analysis of the working of such 'tiers of government' is not possible. This is possible only after certain status-ambiguities are first resolved. Are they instruments of popular democracy for empowerment of the citizens or are they an instrument for better implementation of governance? Is this so-called 'third-tier' an institution of empowerment or an institution of governance? Because of the nature of Indian society, the type of problems that we face, the diversities that exist, and the possibilities of making decisions at that level, it is high time that it is regarded as a third level of government and not just some unit to provide civic amenities.

Even if there is some substance in what has been constitutionally provided to the local-level governments, much of it has been eroded due to compulsions of power-play. Nobody, who has power, wants to surrender it voluntarily and nobody is willing to empower another at own cost. The growth of local-level leadership is perceived as a threat by the entrenched national and state elite. Yet, we talk of local-level governments as instruments of empowerment and governance. In this talk of empowerment, what is overlooked is our own competence to empower 'the lower, the third tier.' It is a condescending approach which assumes that power rightfully belongs only to the Union and the states and they, in their abundant wisdom, have devolved power on the 'third tier,' empowering the local-level governments. The system can work if we accept that power belongs to the people who give it to the next tier upward, and then next tier further upward. In the so-called empowerment of the local-level governments, actually the power gets transferred from one set of elite to another. In the Indian rural power-structure, so much of inequality exists that this empowerment may actually strengthen inequality and oppression.

One of upcoming issues with which Indian federalism would have to deal with is the changing nature of law and order issues and of terrorism. Dealing with new types of law and order situation is no longer possible for any one state. It has become a national issue but there are clear differences between political parties over this. Union's position, while dealing with different states over this issue, is also not above board. For political considerations, the Union remains inactive when some states do not implement this Act and, for different poll considerations, the Union protests its implementation by other states. Cyber crimes, and other types of white-collar crimes, are not limited to boundaries of a state and are national and international issues. There is a federal dimension in dealing with issues that transcend state boundaries: under whose powers is issue of law and order? If the Union intervenes in state boundaries for tackling law and order problems, it would become a contentious issue.

The liberalisation of national economy, and deregulation of the latter, have transformed the state from being a regulator to a facilitator. No doubt, even a federal state would have to regulate, but a facilitating state would regulate differently. It is in this context that the issue of a supposed-paradigm shift needs to be analyzed. Is it because of a deregulation and economic opening up that the Chief Ministers of states are in a position to directly negotiate foreign investment for their states? Or, because of their political clout and the considerations of political coalitions, the Union government allows some of them to so impact on our federal structure and inter-government relations. It is not just a globalised economy that the States' Chief Ministers are in a position to deal directly with other countries. It is due to compulsions of coalition politics and political alliances that the Union conveniently looks the other way. Set conventions are yet to evolve but state governments are establishing their own offices in other countries to attract foreign investment. Is this constitutionally permissible? Were they not part of a ruling coalition, the Union might have taken this as a diversion from constitution and institutional framework of federalism.

There is another problem that comes out of the ongoing 'globalisation' of decisions, policies, services and economics. In the light of the fast-emerging global governance, there may not be any power left to share between different governments within a country. For instance, environmental law and its framing have ceased to be matters of our concern. We are signatories of certain international Protocols and Conventions and we have no option but to implement laws so framed by certain international institutions. Since our options are so limited, it does not matter who shares what or who works. If there is no power left to share, we cannot conceive of sharing powers at union, state and local levels. Once the state as such becomes depoliticised and, subsequently, redundant, then even if powers are decentralised it won't matter.

Federalism does not devote relationships only between a Union and the states, but not much attention has been given to need for cooperation between states. There are no constitution rules governing a relationship between two states, and it is the Union which dictates these relations. There are various issues of conflicts between states, such as river-water distribution, where inter-state cooperation is required just as it is needed for tackling problems of law and order cutting across state boundaries. There is another dimension and equally relevant too. Regional disparities have increased during the last 50 years. It seems that, instead of any lack of decentralisation, it is decentralisation that has made it easier for the states not to discharge responsibilities entrusted to them. They have been given so much to implement that they do not implement at all. Shirking their own responsibilities, states look towards the Union. This aspect of Indian federalism is still not clear. Is it a questions of constitution framework of distribution of powers and responsibilities? Is it due to a lack of funding provided to the states by the Union? Or, whether states have not exercised their responsibilities that they were supposed to do?

The constitutional division of responsibilities between the Centre and the states/ provinces is the basis of a federal structure. Responsibilities of various tiers of government are determined by the functions that are assigned to them. The ability and competence to perform these functions depend on the earmarking of sources of finance. Three factors contributed to an intensification of inter-governmental interaction during the twentieth century: the general trend to increased activity of governments at all levels creating more overlaps, the development of new policy areas such as the environment and energy not contemplated at the time the older federations were designed, and the changing conditions affecting over time the allocations of taxing powers and expenditure responsibilities to different governments and creating vertical and horizontal imbalances. These required intergovernmental transfers and processes and institutions for the periodic adjustment of financial relations among governments. Now as federations move into the twenty-first century, the interdependence inherent within all federal systems is being further extended and complicated by its widened scope increasingly embracing the international and municipal spheres as well.

Comparing any two or more federal systems, we need to look at how power is divided at the centre between the executive and legislative branches, and in terms of area, i.e. between federal, state and municipal levels. There are many reasons why co-ordination is sought. Often, it is useful because programs in different jurisdictions impinge on each other. The system of the division of powers, in the governing structure, depends upon the values that are to be maximised.

Thus, the United States' governmental structure is characterised by checks and balances In the US, with the value preference for maximising the freedom of the individual there is a strict division of power at the centre between the executive (the President) and the legislature (Congress). In terms of an area or geographic division of power, freedom against the constraint of powerful central government was meant to be assured through "states rights" as a countervailing force against the federal government. The textbook description of American government structure has been "separation of institutions but shared powers." But the way the national government of the United States has found to try to exert its authority is through fiscal relationships, another method is legal decisions, and often both. Nowhere does the US Constitution mention local governments, and its legal structure of federalism is "dual," with the states on one end and the nation on the other. The local governments were and remain creatures of the states. In practice, local governments in the US are given importance because of a tradition and philosophy even if they are not "constitutionally" created at the national level, and their legal basis is clearly the state. This is based on the philosophy that any unit whose citizens elect its decision making officials, and gives them authority to enact taxes on those citizens to support it, is a government, whether it is the nation, the states, or the local governments created by the states. Often the county level of government is utilized by states to deliver services as an administrative unit, but the county is also considered a government itself. Efforts in the United States to get local governments to consolidate have mostly failed because of local citizen opposition, with a few notable exceptions where counties and cities have merged. On the other hand, the ability to create highly specific "special districts," which focus on one function such as a utility or capital intensive improvement, has resulted in the expansion of that type of government unit.

In Canada, on the other hand, the value-emphasis is on the maximisation of the welfare or results side. At the centre, in Canada, there is little division of power between the executive (Prime Minister) and the legislature (Parliament). Indeed, under this parliamentary system, the PM's control over his caucus, and hence the legislature, is legendary In fact, the Senate is appointed, virtually for life, by the Prime Minister. Thus, Canada is a federation not by choice, but by necessity. Over decades, the combination of the political power of the provinces, and a string of constitutional court decisions interpreting provincial powers more broadly, has led to a Canada where power is not concentrated at the centre, but is shared more evenly between the provinces and the federal government. The assertiveness of the provinces has led to a federalism that is a collaboration between the provinces and the federal government. The debate in Canada is today less about division of powers and more about recognition of roles and responsibilities.

In Switzerland, the underlying philosophy is that, in order to establish and limit political power, federal constituents must have legitimacy of the great majority of the concerned cultural communities; and this legitimacy can be achieved if the different communities have the power to participate on equal footing in the constitution-making process. Article 2 of the Constitution mandates the Confederation to enhance and promote the cultural diversity. In this way, the federal government gets additional powers and responsibilities, as against the traditional Cantonal competences, in the fields of culture, religion and education. No doubt, Cantons are sovereign in matters of their culture and linguistic policy but these policies have to conform to the limitations of Article 70 wherein the Confederation has the additional responsibility to encourage the understanding among different linguistic communities. According to Article 52 (1) of the **Swiss** Constitution the Confederation shall protect the constitutional order of the cantons. While primary responsibility for ensuring constitutional order lies with the cantons (Article 57 of the Constitution), the Confederation and the other cantons are called to support the concerned canton if it cannot ensure its own constitutional order (*principle of comity*). This duty of support is based on Article 44 (1)-(2) of the Constitution, which states that the Confederation and the cantons shall support each other in the fulfillment of their tasks. A federal intervention is foreseen when the inner order of a canton is disturbed or threatened and cannot be protected by the canton alone or with the help of other cantons (Article 52 (2) of the Constitution).

The 1999 Swiss Constitution places more emphasis on the principle of cooperation than on the principle of self-rule as expressed by the autonomy of the Cantons. This Constitution has introduced three major changes : 1. the right of the Cantons to participate in the foreign policy decisions of the federal government, 2. the general right to participate in internal federal legislation, and 3. the general possibility for Cantons to regulate matters of general concern through inter-cantonal or international treaties. In order to participate in the federal decision-making processes, Cantonal executives created a new body—Council of Presidents of Cantonal Governments—and this has enabled the Cantons to use new ways and means for inter-cantonal partnership and cooperation.

The German federation is the best example of being moulded on cooperative lines. The horizontal division of power, which tends to characterise that system leaves most principal questions of policy to the federation. The states (*Lander*) actively participate in the federal decision making process through their participation in the federal council (*Bundesrat*). Most administration constitutionally is assigned to the sphere of the Lander, through the federal and state bureaucracies that duplicate each other. The court hierarchy reflects these arrangements, providing a single avenue for the resolution of disputes irrespective of the jurisdiction in which they arise.

There are three *levels* of intergovernmental mechanisms in Germany and their main functions are:

- — co-ordination and preparation of voting, and finally voting itself about federal and European legislation at the level of the "federal state"
- — mutual consultation and co-operation in all fields and in particular in overlapping areas of competence at the level of the "Whole state", and
- — co-ordination in the preparation of both Länder and federal legislation as also (and sometimes primarily) on matters of administration on the Third Level.

The entire intergovernmental structure in Germany is governed by the overarching principle of *federal comity* or *loyalty (Bundestreue)*, which permeates all institutional and behavioural emanations of federal practice. It focuses on the demand that both the Federation and the Lander have to take care of "mutual considerateness" in the exercise of their respective powers and that all of their actions and intentions must be "friendly to the idea of federation."

The Constitution of India establishes a rather centralised polity in which the Union government is vested with sufficient powers to ensure not only its dominance, but also its ability to rule in a unitary fashion, if necessary, and politically feasible. Equally important, the country's diversity and socio-economic conditions, coupled with the ideological influences of socialism, drove the Constitution toward a kind of organically unitary federalism in the name of justice, equality, and rights protection. Only a strong centre, thought many of the founders, could effectively drive economic development and ensure equity across territorial jurisdictions, religions, languages, classes, and castes. Hence the trend generally was toward ever more centralisation from independence to the 1980s. At the time of the framing of the Constitution, the impetus for national unity, as represented by the freedom movement, was so strong that the sub-national identities of citizens were given little consideration. Only later was it realised that federalism could help solve conflicts rooted in territorially based ethnic, religious, linguistic, and other characteristics. Since 1989, coalition governments at the Centre, proliferating regional and state parties across the country, and liberalisation of the economy, have served to decentralise the federal political system in many respects.

The Constitution of India establishes a rather centralised polity in which the Union government is vested with sufficient powers to ensure not only its dominance, but also its ability to rule in a unitary fashion, if necessary, and politically feasible. Equally important, the country's diversity and socio-economic conditions, coupled with the ideological influences of socialism, drove the Constitution toward a kind of organically unitary federalism in the name of justice, equality, and rights protection. Only a strong centre, thought many of the founders, could effectively drive economic development and ensure equity across territorial jurisdictions, religions, languages, classes, and castes. Hence the trend generally was toward ever more centralisation, from independence to the 1980s. At the time of the framing of the Constitution, the impetus for national unity, as represented by the freedom movement, was so strong that the sub-national identities of citizens were given little consideration. Only later was it realised that federalism could help solve conflicts rooted in territorially based ethnic, religious, linguistic, and other characteristics. Since 1989, coalition governments at the Centre, proliferating regional and state parties across the country, and liberalisation of the economy, have served to decentralise the federal political system in many respects.

The division of powers between the Union and the states reflects the distribution of responsibilities between them. The Union has been assigned the duty of nation building, maintenance of unity, protection of territorial integrity of the country, and maintenance of constitutional-political order throughout the country. The states are to cooperate with the Union in performing these functions and in discharging their own constitutional duties with regard to local issues. But as soon as any subject ceases to be "local," the Union may intervene to legislate on the matter.

Article 257(1) of the Constitution elaborates that "the executive power of the Union shall extend to the giving of such directions to a state as may appear to the Government of India to be necessary for that purpose." Under this provision, the Union can issue a direction only where some action of a state government is likely to prejudice the exercise of the executive power of the Union. The power of the Union government to give directions to the state governments is fortified by Article 365. If a state government flouts directions provided by the Union government, the president can conclude that "a situation has arisen in which the Government of [a] state cannot be carried on in accordance with the provisions of this Constitution." If one carefully analyses this provision, the operative word appears to be *cannot*, implying an impossibility of governance rather than any difficulty in governance. It is clear that a presidential proclamation under Article 356 is for emergencies; it is not to be made based upon a consideration that is extraneous to the purpose for which the power is conferred — that is, a breakdown of constitutional machinery in a state. Such a provision should not be seen as contrary to the federal principle. For the federal Constitution to function, the Union executive must have the power to give directions to the state executives, as the executive authority of the federation also extends to states.

The Constitution directs that the executive power of every state be so exercised as to ensure compliance with, and not to impede or prejudice, the exercise of the executive power of the Union, and the Union has the power to give such directions to a state as may appear necessary for the purpose of ensuring compliance with Union laws (Art. 256). However, the Supreme Court has held that this does not empower the Union to interfere in any matter pertaining to the exclusive concern of a state. Under article 356, the president may by proclamation assume to himself the executive powers of the state and declare that the powers of the state legislature shall be exercised by or under the authority of the Union Parliament. When a proclamation of emergency is in operation, the Union executive is empowered to give directions to any state on how the executive power thereof is to be exercised.

However, in 1994 the Supreme Court held that the Court can examine whether the president issued a proclamation based on bad faith *(mala fides)* or on irrelevant considerations because the Court is not precluded from calling upon the Union government to disclose to the Court the material upon which the president formed his or her judgement. In this way, the Court sought to contain the Union government's attempts to ride roughshod over the states by threatening them with dismissal.

The status of the states under the Constitution can be summed up as follows:

1. The Constitution does not grant to any state the right of secession.
2. The states have no *a priori* rights or powers but

only rights or powers and competences expressly granted to them by the Constitution. Even the residual powers are vested in the Union government. In the field of concurrent powers, Union law prevails over a state law that conflicts with a Union law.

3. There is a single constitution for both the Union and the states. No state has the right to adopt its own constitution. Part VI of the Constitution provides the framework for the government of the states.
4. There is a single unified judiciary for the whole country and an integrated civil service under the supervision and control of the All-India Services.
5. There is a single citizenship for the people of the country and no separate citizenship for the people of any state.
6. The governors of states are appointees of the Union government (i.e., of the president), and besides being the constitutional head of state, a governor also is the eyes and ears of the Union in the state.
7. The Constitution guarantees individual rights and rights of certain groups, such as scheduled castes, scheduled tribes, and minorities, but not of states as such. It does not concede even the right of equal representation to the states in the upper house of the Union Parliament.

What is now called competition in India's negotiated federalism actually developed as a result of the emergence of coalition politics and power sharing. In this way, the Union and the states under the impact of competitive party politics and increasing regionalism have become more like coordinate centres of power. Howsoever strong the position of the Union in planning, programming, and financing, the execution of plans and projects rests in the hands of the state governments. No other large federal government is as dependent as India's on theoretically subordinate, but actually rather distinct, units responsible to a different order of government for so much of the administration of what are recognised as national programs. In the final analysis, the authority organically exercised in New Delhi is influence rather than power.

Federal systems require inter-governmental processes and institutions for tackling the unavoidable questions concerning overlapping jurisdictions.

There are many variations among these federations in their institutional design, the character of the diversity within their societies, their degree of economic development, and their policy agendas. Nevertheless a common feature among them has been the need for effective internal intergovernmental arrangements. Thus, while there is no single federal model or example that is applicable everywhere, there is much to be gained from examining the similarities and differences in their approaches to facilitating federal-provincial and inter-provincial cooperation and co-ordination. Since many of the problems are common to virtually all federations, examining the experience of other federations in institutionalising intergovernmental relations may provide us with both positive and negative lessons, i.e. with both effective examples and cautionary tales.

In most of the contemporary states and societies, certain federal practices can be instruments not just of good governance but also of conflict management. They include power-sharing, people's participation, devolution of power and authority, and inter-governmental collaboration. This is particularly so in plural societies— that form an overwhelming majority in the international community. In such societies, issues of unity with diversity, self-rule and peaceful resolution of contentious issues, between tiers of government, have attracted attention and growing interest of scholars and practitioners of federalism.

The need for intergovernmental collaborative institutions and processes, has led to an emphasis upon 'cooperative federalism' within most federations, although the extent of this has varied greatly from those where duality and exclusivity of powers have been strongly emphasized to those where shared and concurrent jurisdiction have received greater emphasis.

In this framework, there are clear-cut policy options to facilitate smooth inter-governmental relations, in India.

The starting point has to be adding to the competence of the Inter State Council (ISC). Since the ISC is an advisory body, it is difficult to assess the efficacy of its policy performance. And, for the same reason, its cost-effectiveness also cannot be determined. A solid institutional structure for inter-governmental cooperation has not emerged. In its functioning it has remained only an adjunct, an annexe, of the Ministry of Home Affairs. Even after its establishment, the ISC has not been able to attract sufficient attention from the state governments. With the Central government becoming weak..... different political parties ruling at the Union and in several states, and the Central government enjoying the majority support in the Parliament without any party being in majority..... and due to exigencies of coalition politics, the Central governments had to share power. The bargaining power of the states with the Union has markedly increased and they no longer need a mechanism like the ISC to bargain with the Union.

Accordingly, the ISC needs to be included in the process of central legislation over matters in state list. In such cases, not only informal consultations between the

Union and the states should be there, but also the central government should place the proposal before the ISC before such a legislation is introduced.

The jurisdictional competence of the ISC needs to be extended so as to enable it to review every bill of national importance or which is likely to affect the interests of one or more states before it is introduced in the Parliament or a state Assembly. There should be no limitation on the ISC that it can consider only political issues.

The Union's directions to a state government, under any of the Articles, ought be issued in consultation with, and with the approval of, the Inter-state Council. Since the purpose of the setting up of the ISC was to facilitate the Union in its coordination activities, it cannot discharge its function without being a body for securing cooperation between two levels of government as well.

Most of the inter-governmental tensions and conflict emerge over fiscal issues, though there are constitutional mechanisms provided for such contingencies. However, the constitutional arrangements have not been objectively operated upon and, instead, the financial transfers have been politicised. In view of this, it would be worthwhile to consider a mechanism for recommending fiscal transfers by some independent body working under the auspices of the ISC. The latter needs to determine the quantum of central assistance to states and its inter-state distribution. In view of the fact that over 60 per cent of resource transfers from the Union to the states are made through the Planning Commission and the central government's ministries, and not via the Finance Commission (which is an statutory body), it is hardly surprising that the Union's intervention in the states' development programmes has so much increased. It needs to be pointed out that issues of economic planning and development cannot be settled through institutions set up be the Union government, such as Planning and Finance Commissions. They require coordinated efforts and for that cooperated federal arrangements are needed, which role can best be provided by concerted ventures of National Development Council and the Inter state Council. The possibility of the Inter-state Council and the National Development Council merging into a common inter-governmental forum deserves serious consideration by constitutional experts and policy-makers.

In CONCLUSION it may be pointed out that instruments of inter-governmental cooperation have not been successful and effective because the required decentralization has not been made. This is mainly due to India's administrative centralization and earlier central planning structures.. A mechanism for inter-governmental cooperation can succeed if it does not have to depend on other executive organizations for getting its decisions implemented. In the debates on federalism, special attention needs to be given—but often is not given—to the importance of inter-governmental relations and mechanisms for resolving contentious issues between different tiers of government. Inter-governmental agencies have generally operated outside the framework of the Constitution. At least in India, the inter-governmental agencies have not acquired the functional relevance visualized in the Constitution. The recommendations of inter-governmental agencies, in India, have lacked any force and have not been in a position to cope with the inter-jurisdictional strains of the Indian federal set-up. This is due to the ad hoc style of their functioning and this has eroded their credibility. Cooperative federalism can succeed only if a fair balance is maintained between the claims of diversity and the requirements of unity. If that is absent, whatever mechanisms of inter-governmental relations are devised would remain non-functional and ineffective.

The Indian Constitution would seem, in the end, to create a 'cooperative union' of states rather than a dual polity. What is being observed now is federal restructuring through politically developed rules and conventions, without disturbing the basic scheme of the Constitution. The actual working of cooperative federalism in India has entailed the Union's exercising its influence rather than its constitutional authority. Exigencies of coalition politics have forced the Union and state governments to share power. The Union has more often played the role of a facilitator in interstate disputes than that of an arbitrator. A redistribution of powers—through decentralisation and the devolution of authority from the Union to the states and from the states to the panchayats and municipalities—is serving to facilitate the attainment of the objectives of the Constitution: unity, social justice, and democracy. Any federal system is a device of shared-governance, and the Constitution of India envisages a 'creative balance' between the need for an effective Union and effectively empowered states. A healthy sign is the growing realisation that inter-governmental relations need to focus more on the needs of the citizens—particularly in welfare policy areas—rather than on questions of turf and jurisdiction. The debate is today less about division of powers and more about recognition of roles and responsibilities. Federal governance is a mechanism that is suitable to countries like India where there are different levels of development and different levels of resources available. For that, some power sharing is required in the system of governance. For that sense of accommodation to be there, a paradigm shift is needed in which democracy need not be just representative but a participatory democracy.

Further Readings

Banting, Keith and T.J. Courchene, *The Future of Fiscal Federalism*, (Kingston: School of Policy Studies, Queen's University Press, 1987).

Burgess, Michael and Alain G. Gagnon, (eds.), *Comparative Federalism and Federation*, (Toronto: University of Toronto Press, 1993).

Brown-John, C.Lloyd, (ed.), *Centralizing and Decentralizing Trends in Federal States*, (London: University Press of America, 1988).

Burges, Michael and Alain-G, Gagnon, (eds.), *Comparative Federalism and Federation: Competing Trends and Future Directions*, (Hemel Hempstead: Harvester Wheatsheaf, 1993).

De Villiers, Bertus, (ed.), *Evaluating Federal Systems*, (Cape Town: Jutta & Co., 1994).

Elazar, Daniel J., (ed.), *Federal Systems of the World: A Hanbook of Federal*, Confederal and Autonomy Arrangements, 2nd (ed.), (Harlow: Longman Group Limited, 1994).

Franks, C.E.S., *Parliament, Intergovernmental Relations, and National Unity*, (Kingston, Queen's University: Institute for Intergovernmental Relations, 1999[a]).

Franks, C.E.S., J.E. Hodgetts, O.P. Dwivedi, Doug Williams, and V. Seymour Wilson, (eds.), *Canada's Century: Governance in a Maturing Society*, (Montreal and Kingston: McGill-Queen's University Press, 1995[a]).

Galligan, Brian, *A Federal Republic: Australia's Constitutional System of Government*, (Oakleigh, Melbourne: Cambridge University Press, 1995).

Jeffery, C., (ed.), *Recasting German Federalism*, (London and New York: Pinter, 1999).

Majeed, Akhtar, *Federalism Within the Union*, (New Delhi: Manak, 2004).

Majeed, Akhtar, Ronald Watts and Douglas Brown, *Distribution of Responsibilities in Federal Polities*, (Montreal: Queens University, 2006)

Simiely, Donald V. and R.L. Wattts, *Intrastate Federalism in Canada,* (Toronto: University of Toronto Press, 1985).

Verney, Douglas V., "Federalism, Federative Systems, and Federations: The United States, Canada and India," *Publius: The Journal of Federalism,* 25:2 (1995): 81-97.

7

Fiscal Dependence of the States of India on the Union

Inter-governmental fiscal transfers are common in all the federations especially because of the often unavoidable asymmetry in the assignment of powers and functions among governments and uneven economic development causing wide disparities in fiscal capabilities in constituent units.

One of the purposes of intergovernmental co-operation in Australia is to secure financial assistance. Revenue redistribution has been a feature of the Australian federation for most of the time since the Constitution came into effect. From the outset, the grants power in section 96 of the Australian Constitution has provided the mechanism through which re-distribution might occur. It allows the Commonwealth Parliament to grant financial assistance to any state 'on such terms and conditions as thinks fit.' By determining the conditions attached to such grants, the Commonwealth can achieve, through the states, many of its own policy goals. Under current arrangements, more than $AUD 50 billion is transferred from the Commonwealth to the states each year. The total transferred is divided roughly equally between general revenue and specific purpose grants. Specific purpose grants provide the states with all or part of the revenue to fund programs in areas of state responsibility including health, education and housing. They also provide an avenue through which Commonwealth policy is given effect in these areas, despite the absence of any other constitutional power.

The leading German institutions in the field of financial co-ordination are:

The Finance Committee of the Bundesrat, being the only one of its committees in which the Ministers of the Länder regularly participate in person (while in the others business is mostly delegated to civil servants), the Financial Planning Commission, consisting of the federal Ministers of Finance and of Economic Affairs, the Finance Ministers of the Länder plus four representatives of the local government bodies (the municipalities and the counties) and the Finance Ministers' Conference of the Länder.

From its origin in the federal Constitution of 1891, the Brazilian federation adopted a system of separate tax sources, distinguishing taxes for which the states had the exclusive competence from those of the federal government. Municipal governments only acquired exclusive competence to implement taxes after the 1934 Constitution. In the current system, tax collection is very concentrated: the five main taxes are accountable for more than 70 per cent of total tax collection – four of them are collected by the federal government. The most important tax is collected by the states: Imposto sobre Circulação de Mercadorias e Serviços – ICMS (state Value Added Tax). Constitutional transfers distribute part of the revenue collected by the federal government to states and municipalities, and from states to their respective municipalities. On the vertical plane, the current fiscal transfer system allows almost all relative income to be appropriated by municipal governments, since their results are neutral for the states). Furthermore, this system favours small size municipalities. On the horizontal plane, this system redistributes revenue from more developed to less developed states even though constitutional transfer rules have the consequence of creating new inequalities among Federative Units. Therefore, the Brazilian system for tax revenue sharing is essentially a legal, by which tax revenue with no compulsory spending allocation – except for constitutional obligations in health and education spending – is ensured to sub-national governments, notably small size municipalities. The result of this redistribution is a significant horizontal inequality in spending capacity of sub-national governments.

In the United States, states have plenary power to tax and local governments may tax those activities and set rates within the discretion authorized by the states. The national government collects most of its direct taxes with the income tax. In practice, the states have tended to utilize sales taxes, with income taxes also used. Local governments historically have utilized a tax on real property, but throughout the nation there is great variety in other forms of taxes including income taxes.

All three levels of government, in Switzerland, may raise taxes. The citizens pay about one third of their taxes to each level of government. According to Article 127 (1) of the Constitution, the general principles of taxation—particularly the circle of taxpayers, the object of the tax and its calculation—shall be established by statute. The tax scales, tax rates and tax exempt amounts are decided either by a cantonal parliament or by popular cantonal referendum without intervention of the federal level. Federal harmonization can only concern tax liability, tax object, taxation period, and procedural and criminal law on taxation.

An important feature of India's financial framework is revenue sharing between the Union and the states. Finally, Parliament is empowered to make such grants as it deems necessary to providing financial assistance for any state in need. Such grants can be block grants or specific categorical grants. There is a clear vertical imbalance between (1) the powers of taxation assigned to the Union and the states and (2) the social and economic responsibilities assigned to the states. That is, the states' responsibilities exceed their own-source revenues. But, the Finance Commission, the Planning Commission, and the National Development Council provide mechanisms for periodically correcting this imbalance and for allowing the states to better discharge their responsibilities. These forums cater to the grievances of the states, which they redress to the extent possible.

Issues of Fiscal Federalism have been thorny though inter-governmental jurisdiction over taxation has been clearly demarcated in the Union and the State Lists in the VIIth Schedule of the Constitution. These constitutional arrangements have not been objectively operated upon and instead the financial transfers have been politicised. In view of the fact that over 60 per cent of resource transfers from the Centre to the states are made through the Planning Commission and the Central government's ministries, and not via the Finance Commission, it is hardly surprising that central intervention in the states' development programmes has so much increased. The Sarkaria Commission had also discussed setting up an expert committee to recommend restructuring taxation and resource distribution from the Centre to the states. It was proposed that an advisory Sub-Committee of Finance be set up in the National Development Council, and that the Finance Commission itself work under the member incharge of financial resources in the Planning Commission. It needs to be pointed out that issues of economic planning and development cannot be settled through institutions set up be the central government, such as Planning and Finance Commissions. They require coordinated efforts and for that cooperated federal arrangements are needed, which role can best be provided by concerted ventures of National Development council and the Inter state Council.

Entry 20 of the Concurrent List (VIIth Schedule) of the Constitution empowers both the Union and the states to legislate on economic and social planning, and there are a number of subjects in the States' list which are relevant to planning. Since the union law prevails in the event of jurisdiction dispute between the Union and the states, the Union can go to any extent in the name of planning. In many of the spheres of state activity, the Union government has stepped in, not through any constitutional provision but, through the process of administration. In matters of implementation of plan policies in areas of land-reforms, forest development, development of rural industries, irrigation, cooperative farming, agriculture, education, health, cottage industries etc, the Planning Commission insists on uniform policies to be followed by the states. It is believed that though the primary responsibility in such matters is of state governments, the Union has an overall responsibility for helping coordinate and guide the work of the states so that national policies can be satisfactorily worked out.

Though the Constitution had established a territorial

federation, a vertical federation has emerged because of the process and style of planning. Under Art. 282 of the Constitution, Plan grants are given by the Union to the states in the form of matching grants. Actually, various ministries of the government of India issue grants to corresponding ministries of state governments and, in this way, they are in a position to dictate and supervise departments of state governments. A vertical federation has resulted in which, through matching grants, the departments of Union and state governments on the same subject form a unit for the purposes of programmes and expenditure on the same. The state level bodies are merely implementing bodies and not the ones to consider the policies on the same level for the state as the Planning Commission does for the whole country. By allowing the Union to tighten its financial grip over the states, the planning method and process has introduced a political complexion in the relationship between the Union and the states. Grants provided to the states on the recommendations of the Finance Commission are made under Art. 275 of the Constitution, and those on the recommendations of the Planning Commission under Art. 282. When the Union government provides grants, under Art. 275, through the Finance Commission, there is a constitutional obligation and hence it does not add to the authority of the Centre. But grants, under Art. 282, through the Planning Commission are discretionary and, therefore, political in nature. Something that is not good for the smooth functioning of the federal system is the upward trend of grants through Planning Commission and a slower rate of growth of grants through the Finance Commission. It not only increases financial dependence of states on the Union, it also reduces the Finance Commission, which is an objective federal body, to relative insignificance. At one of the meetings of the Inter-state Council, it was recommended that taxation should be transferred to the Concurrent List. State autonomy would be greatly affected by the performance-linking of central-plan assistance and Finance Commission's awards. In spite of being contrary to the Constitutional provisions, this attack on the federal structure has not been given proper attention.

The Planning Commission gives a continuum of discretionary grants to the states under Art 282 of the Constitution: "The Union or a state may make grants for any public purpose, notwithstanding that the purpose is not one with respect to which Parliament or the legislature of the state may make laws." Under this discretionary provision, plan grants are made on a regular basis. All this can be rectified if the Finance Commission determines plan assistance and the Planning Commission looks after planning and statutory devolutions. The Administrative Reforms Commission (ARC) had earlier recommended that the Finance Commission should determine grants as well as plan assistance and, for better coordination, a member of the Planning Commission may be appointed to the Finance Commission also.

Reviewing the functioning and the actual powers exercised by the Planning Commission, Mr M.C. Setalwad, India's first Attorney General, had once remarked that it was somewhat anamolous that "vast resources should be devolved to the states by the Union at the instance of a purely executive body." The need to review the role and powers of the Planning Commission is as relevant today as it was when the above statement was made. Much later, Dr P.V. Rajamannar, Chairman of the Fourth Finance Commission (1964), noting that the policy and programmes of the Plan come within the purview of the Planning Commission, had observed that the assistance to be given by the Centre for plan projects is practically dependent on the recommendations of the Planning Commission and, therefore, a body like the Finance Commission cannot operate in the same field. He had recommended that the Planning Commission be made a statutory body, independent of the government. It does look rather odd that, in practice, it exercises more powers than the Finance Commission which has been set up by the Constitution. Through the Planning Commission, the Centre has not only controlled the state sector of the Plan but also their implementation.

The Planning Commission gives a continuum of discretionary grants to the states under Art. 282 of the Constitution:

The Union or a state may make grants for any public purpose, notwithstanding that the purpose is not one with respect to which Parliament or the legislature of the state may make laws." Under this discretionary provision, plan grants are made on a regular basis. All this can be rectified if the Finance Commission determines plan assistance and the Planning Commission looks after planning and statutory devolutions. The Administrative Reforms Commission (ARC) had earlier recommended that the Finance Commission should determine grants as well as plan assistance and, for better coordination, a member of the Planning Commission may be appointed to the Finance Commission also.

The Finance Commission cannot make recommendations on grants-in-aid (Art. 275) and on discretionary grants (Art. 282). These grants are within the jurisdiction of the Planning Commission. Over the years, plan grants have gone on increasing. The states have been demanding greater role for the Finance Commission as against the Planning Commission on the plea that the latter is a political body and is likely to be susceptible to the Central government.

With the introduction of economic liberalization and the 'New Economic Policy,' it seems that now the Centre also shares the views of the states on this point. With the increasing 'dis-investment' and withdrawl from various fields of activity, the Central government is bound to reduce the role of the Planning Commission. In the fiscal sphere, it may force the states towards competitive performance and then the resultant gap in inter-state disparities.

There has been a perception among various state governments that their aspirations are not reflected in the plans of the National Development Council (NDC) and the Planning Commission. This is so because the level of consultations in the NDC is not adequate and there is too much of interference by the Planning Commission in programmes falling within state jurisdiction. Zonal Councils have been insignificant both in resolution of conflicts and in coordinating state policies. Many of the state governments feel that harmonious relationship is possible in the presence of institutional consultation and consensus-making. However, it was the centralized nature of Indian federalism that ensured that the institutionalized mechanisms of cooperative federalism do not develop. The over-centralization of the decision-making process and the dis-institutionalization of inter-governmental relations has gone hand in hand. There has been a singular lack of confidence among the states in centrally dominated institutions of cooperative federalism. It is not altogether misplaced also because more often innovations in institutionalized inter-governmental relations have only replicated the institutions they were supposed to improve upon. The perception is not entirely baseless that there has been a trivialization of formal mechanisms such as the NDC and the ISC.

This fiscal anemology is not a case in isolation. There are various transgressions of constitutional distribution of powers, of competences and jurisdictions that are against the spirit of federalism; and a comprehensive debate is needed to clear the mist over statutory propriety.

Further Readings

Adenduer, Konrad Foundation, *State Local Fiscal Relations in India,* (New Delhi: Manohar, 1998).

Chaubey, P.K., *Fiscal Federalism in India,* (New Delhi: Deep & Deep, 2001).

Rao, Hemlata, *Fiscal Federalism,* (New Delhi: New Century, 2006).

Singh, Udai Bhan, *Fiscal Federalism in Indian Union,* (New Delhi: Concept, 2003).

Suri, M.M., *Centre-State Financial Relations in India,* (New Delhi: New Century, 2008).

Vithal, B.P.R. and M.L. Sastry, *Fiscal Federalism in India,* (New Delhi: Oxford, 2001).

8

Inter-Governmental Conflict Resolution

Inter-governmental conflict is manifest in a federal state. Such a conflict cannot be avoided and has to be managed. It is part of both the shared rule and self rule.

The constitutional division of responsibilities between the Centre and the states/ provinces is the basis of a federal structure. Responsibilities of various tiers of government are determined by the functions that are assigned to them. The ability and competence to perform these functions depend on the earmarking of sources of finance. In Indian, three factors contributed to an intensification of inter-governmental interaction during the twentieth century: the general trend to increased activity of governments at all levels creating more overlaps, the development of new policy areas such as the environment and energy not contemplated at the time the older federations were designed, and the changing conditions affecting over time the allocations of taxing powers and expenditure responsibilities to different governments and creating vertical and horizontal imbalances. These required inter-governmental transfers and processes and institutions for the periodic adjustment of financial relations among governments. Now as we move into the twenty-first century, the interdependence inherent within all federal systems is being further extended and complicated by its widened scope increasingly embracing the international and municipal spheres as well.

Federal systems require inter-governmental processes and institutions for tackling the unavoidable questions concerning overlapping jurisdictions.

There are many variations among the federations in their institutional design, the character of the diversity within their societies, their degree of economic development, and their policy agendas. Nevertheless a common feature among them has been the need for effective internal intergovernmental arrangements. Thus, while there is no single federal model or example that is applicable everywhere, there is much to be gained from examining the similarities and differences in their approaches to facilitating federal-provincial and inter-provincial cooperation and co-ordination. Since many of the problems are common to virtually all federations, examining the experience of other federations in institutionalising intergovernmental relations may provide us with both positive and negative lessons, i.e. with both effective examples and cautionary tales.

In most of the contemporary states and societies, certain federal practices can be instruments not just of good governance but also of conflict management. They include power-sharing, people's participation, devolution of power and authority, and inter-governmental collaboration. This is particularly so in plural societies— that form an overwhelming majority in the international community. In such societies, issues of unity with diversity, self-rule and peaceful resolution of contentious issues, between tiers of government, have attracted attention and growing interest of scholars and practitioners of federalism.

The need for intergovernmental collaborative institutions and processes, has led to an emphasis upon 'cooperative federalism' within most federations, although the extent of this has varied greatly from those where duality and exclusivity of powers have been strongly emphasized to those where shared and concurrent jurisdiction have received greater emphasis.

In Australia, many mechanisms used for co-operative purposes are ordinary tools for governance. Most obviously, they include legislation and co-ordination through informal consultation and agreement. There are some specific mechanisms as well, however, which may be used individually or in combination. These include the mechanisms in the Constitution itself. A referral of power by the states to the Commonwealth under Section 51 (xxxvii) achieves absolute uniformity of legislation and administration. Section 96 enables the Commonwealth to control the expenditure of financial assistance it has given to the states, which it might not otherwise been able to do.. In addition to these, there are two other mechanisms, which are familiar in connection with co-operative schemes, but which are not specifically recognised by the Constitution. These are ministerial councils, and inter-governmental agreements. Australia has a network of ministerial councils, with the Council of Australian Governments (COAG) at its apex, covering almost all areas of government activity. Ministerial councils and their supporting standing committees of officials play a key role in collaborative arrangements. They provide a forum for exchange of information and foster acquaintance between ministers with similar responsibilities in different parts of the country.

Ministerial councils are likely to have responsibility for negotiating new arrangements or revising old ones. Typically, decisions of ministerial councils require unanimity; increasingly however, a form of majority voting is used, the details of which vary between different schemes.

Most significant co-operative arrangements are formalised through an inter-governmental agreement. A formal agreement is signed by the heads of government or by the responsible ministers. An agreement may establish a ministerial council. Typically, agreements set out the essential terms of the co-operative arrangement in issue, including its purpose, decision-making procedures and duration Generally, agreements are not enforceable, either as law or contracts, although exceptions are possible, depending on their terms.

In Canada, Federal-Provincial meetings and conferences involving Ministers, Deputy Ministers and senior officials are organised some 500 times in a year. Departments of Intergovernmental Affairs respond to the need to conduct and manage this activity. The size of these offices vary in accordance with the size of the individual governments and the degree to which they feel the need to project their special interests. Offices vary from one or two individuals within a Premier's Office or Cabinet Office with responsibilities to coordinate central intergovernmental relations involving the First Minister principally to the other extreme of full departments monitoring all intergovernmental contacts and having legislative authority over all intergovernmental agreements. Centrally, a special purpose secretariat was set up to service the process of constitutional review; it had its mandate extended to provide support services to all First Ministers meetings and now services Ministers and Deputy Ministers meetings on sectoral issues. The secretariat is financed on an intergovernmental funding formula with the federal government paying half and the balance being divided among the provinces on a per capita basis. Whereas First Ministers meetings are chaired solely by the Prime Minister and are convened at his choosing, other Ministerial meetings tend to occur at a regular frequency. Some are chaired only by the federal Minister, such as meetings of Ministers of Finance, while others are co-chaired federally and provincially, and agendas are set by consultation.

It was announced, in July 2003, a new formal Interprovincial Council of the Federation. This is comprised of the 13 premiers of the ten provinces and three territories, and will meet on a regular basis. The primary focus of this new council is to serve as a provincial-territorial coordinating body. However, in announcing its formation, the premiers agreed upon the need for annual first ministers' meetings, co-chaired by the Prime Minister and the chair of the Council of the Federation, with agendas jointly determined on such standing items as health, trade, finance, justice and the economy.

In the United States, federal and state political leaders often have different priorities and perspectives, bringing about conflict in the actual exercise of power. Since the mid-1960s, there has been relatively little conflict about the substance of federal policy initiatives. Most state political leaders have come to accept the broad scope of federal authority and rarely challenge the exercise of federal power. Conflict is much more about the manner in which federal power is exercised. However, federal and state political leaders often have different priorities and perspectives, bringing about conflict in the actual exercise of power. Since the mid-1960s, there has been relatively little conflict about the substance of federal policy initiatives. Most state political leaders have come to accept the broad scope of federal authority and rarely challenge the exercise of federal power. Conflict is much more about the manner in which federal power is exercised.

However, there is no national government agency which has the task of coordinating federalism or intergovernmental relationships. While there is constant day to day interaction between local and state officials with each other and their national counterparts, it tends to occur within the subject matter agencies of government, e.g. agriculture, urban affairs, housing, healthcare, and so forth. When there are problems of communication or disagreements about priorities, states and local governments may resort to political contacts with elected representatives, sometimes political party officials, lobbying efforts by their associations, and in some unusual but important cases, even going to the courts of law. At one time there was a national agency entitled the "Advisory Commission on Intergovernmental Relations," but it was discontinued in 1996 for lack of funding. It was not an operating agency and had no coordinating powers in any case. It did a good job of gathering information on intergovernmental fiscal and other matters, and in providing a forum for discussion of matters involving federalism by members from all levels. But the discontinuation of that particular agency in no way has diminished the continuing communications between levels of government on a daily basis.

The US system tends to minimize the importance of formal meetings called to bring together officials of different levels of government because for practical purposes such relationships are a constant part of the daily political and governmental life, ongoing at all times and in many different forums. Formal institutional meetings for discussion purposes are viewed as largely ceremonial. In the recent past, Presidents, Governors, and cabinet officials at both levels have designated certain staff assistants for "Intergovernmental Relations." They are few in number, and limited in authority, and function primarily to advise their principals on intergovernmental matters, and in some cases as a conduit for officials at other levels to communicate with executives or their functional administrators.

The United States' federalism has developed several mechanisms to manage the conflict that is characteristic of the system. These mechanisms may be legal, political or administrative. Except for the judiciary, all of these mechanisms are extra-constitutional. Some are informal while others are institutionalized. In recent years, most Presidents have appointed a special assistant for intergovernmental affairs and charged him with pursuing the President's intergovernmental agenda and with hearing issues raised by the states. State governors are often articulate spokespersons for state interests in the distribution of powers and responsibilities in American federalism. Individually, governors, working with the state's congressional delegation, can have an impact on how specific federal programs are structured and implemented. Collectively, the governors are organized into the National Governors Association (NGA). The NGA's main office is in Washington, D.C. and it attempts to present a unified position on issues that affect state interests. Because of the diversity of the states, the NGA works on a consensus principle and takes stands on issues only when there is near unanimity among the governors. Also because of this diversity, the governors are organized into two partisan organizations, the Democrat Governors Association and the Republican Governors Association, and a number of regional organizations, such as the Western Governors Association, the Southern Governors Association, the Coalition of Northeastern Governors, and the Midwestern Governors Conference.

Members of state legislatures are organized into the National Conference of state Legislatures(NCSL), which lobbies Congress and the federal executive on behalf of state interests. Because of the diversity of its membership, it is often difficult for the NCSL to take a united stand on issues.

While the role of the US Supreme Court is especially crucial, all federal courts play an important role in resolving federal-state conflicts. While these conflicts sometimes raise constitutional issues regarding the proper exercise of federal or state authority, they are even more likely to involve questions of statutory interpretation, or the legality and appropriateness of administrative procedures. In recognition of the important role of the courts in resolving federal-state conflicts, a state and Local legal Center was created in 1983 to help prepare state attorneys for their court appearances, and to submit amicus briefs in federalism cases.

Beginning in the 1970s, state-federal judicial councils were formed in most of the states and charged with the responsibility to "maintain continuing communication on all joint problems," and mitigate the "friction between state and federal courts." While these joint councils addressed some practical problems, such as the coordination of court calendars, few even exist today. A National state-federal Council was created in 1992, but that body also lapsed into desuetude. State judges continue to serve on the major committees of the federal Judicial Conference. The federal-state Jurisdiction Committee of the Judicial Conference is especially relevant because it is primarily concerned with developing recommendations about legislation affecting state and federal jurisdiction, and attempts to promote state-federal judicial cooperation generally.

Far more important for the resolution of federal state judicial conflict in the USA is the National Center for state Courts (NCSC), which brings together the Council of [state]

Chief Justices (CCJ), the Conference of state Court Administrators (COSCA), other state trial and appellate judges, and which provides information to Congress and the federal judiciary on issues of concern to state judiciaries.

There are some informal mechanisms, in the USA, that affect the actual way the system of intergovernmental relations works within the federal system.

Professional Networks of Influence are used by those serving as administrators in government who have professional training in some discipline, for example, engineering, and they may have more in common with their fellow engineers, even though serving at three different government levels, than they do with their fellow employees at their own level. This professional allegiance among those in functional areas of government such as health, agriculture, urban development, social service, or law enforcement is strong on a "vertical" basis in the US. Alliances among elected officials are associations of elected officials that maintain permanent offices, employ specialized officers, are funded from taxes at the level of the members, and that both inform the members and exert influence on those at higher levels of decision making within the system. Some of the national organizations which are not provided for in the Constitution or the law but which express the opinions, on behalf of their citizens, of many different types of official for many different types of government are: National Governors Association, National Conference of state Legislative Officials, Council of state Governments, National Association of County Officials, National League of Cities, US Conference of Mayors, National Association of Towns and Townships.

Political Parties provide Informal Intergovernmental Communications and Influencing Mechanisms. Because of the electoral form in the US which encourages voters to choose between two major parties, those parties often become channels for political decision making that allow interests that get blocked at one governmental level to find receptivity at other levels. Lobbyists and Lobbying Organizations for Specific Interests are used by economic or programme interests who do not succeed at one level to move their advocacy to another level. Now, New Federalism has become a technique for the assertion of state interests for states to work together on a voluntary basis to accomplish policy ends such as the pact among state Attorneys General to seek damages for the states from tobacco companies for the costs incurred for health care. This resulted in a settlement in which states enjoy significant financial benefits, but not from the national government.

In Germany, the management centre of the Bundesrat has its highly efficient Secretariat, consisting mainly of the staff of its departmentally organised committees, who have permanent and very close working relations with the corresponding ministries of both the Länder and the Federation. The efficient performance of the Bundesrat's numerous functions would hardly be possible, however, if that federal body were not surrounded by a circle of Länder institutions, which are very typical of the German structure: All of the Länder have Missions (Vertretungen) to the Federation in Berlin serving liaison functions between the Länder governments on the one side and the parliamentary and governmental organs of the Federation on the other. In doing so they mainly focus on the Bundesrat.

The leading institution for inter-governmental conflict resolution, in Germany, is the Conference of the Heads of Governments of the Federation and the Länder, which is regularly (every three or four months) convened and chaired by the federal Chancellor after preparatory conferences of the Heads of the Cabinet Offices on both levels. Unlike business in the Bundesrat structure, the agendas here are not restricted to matters under federal jurisdiction only, which means that the Conference can discuss any matter of political relevance oft the federal system.. Preparatory and other management functions for the Conference are performed by the federal Chancellor's Office. Particularly in this field it works in close contact with the Cabinet Offices (or state Chancelleries – Staatskanzleien) of the Länder.

In Switzerland disputes among Cantons and Confederation are seldom resolved by court decision. They are decided on a political level either by negotiation or by legislative or constitutional decisions. Comity as guiding line for conflict management has always influenced cantonal and federal authorities in their behavior. This principle requires respect, tolerance and good faith on both levels. Article 47 of the Constitution requires explicitly federal authorities to respect cantonal autonomy. The cantons can decide on the organization of their territory on the setup of institutions, and how those institutions operate. They can limit their own cantonal powers or they can delegate part of their powers to districts or municipalities. Article 44 of the Constitution provides that Confederation and Cantons shall support each other in the fulfillment of their tasks. They owe each other respect and support. With regard to the respect of cantonal autonomy, Article 47 of the Constitution requires the Confederation explicitly to respect cantonal autonomy. Disputes between the Cantons or between Cantons and the Confederation shall as far as is possible, be resolved through negotiation. The concept of Bundestreue has been developed by the constitutional court for Germany. In Switzerland disputes among Cantons and Confederation are seldom resolved by court decision. They are decided on a political level either by negotiation or by legislative or constitutional decisions. Comity as guiding line for conflict management has always influenced cantonal and federal authorities in their behavior. This principle requires respect, tolerance and good faith on both levels. Article 47 of the Constitution requires explicitly federal authorities to respect cantonal autonomy.

Switzerland has a distinctive form of federal executive. The federal Council is a collegial body elected by the federal legislature for a fixed term and composed of seven councilors among whom the presidency rotates annually. This form of executive is also paralleled at the cantonal level. This distinctive institutional arrangement, the tradition of representing all four of the major political parties in the federal Council, the absence of a prohibition of dual membership in the cantonal and federal legislatures, and the constitutional provision making all federal legislation potentially vulnerable to a referendum challenge, have over the years contributed to a tradition of extensive federal-cantonal consultation and negotiation. Under the new constitution adopted in 1999, no formal intergovernmental councils were established. Articles 44-49, however, set out principles of federal-cantonal collaboration, including provision for the cantons to participate in decision-making processes at the federal level including federal legislation (article 45(1)), and requiring federal consultation of the cantons (article 45(2)). The new constitution also specifically provides for the participation of cantons in federal decisions on foreign policy (article 55) and for cantonal treaties with foreign countries in areas within cantonal jurisdiction (article 56). To facilitate inter-cantonal cooperation, the new constitution also specifically permits cantons to enter into inter-cantonal treaties and to create common organizations and institutions (article 48). Also at numerous other points in the new constitution, there are specific references to the requirement of federal-cantonal consultation or collaboration. As a result of these provisions federal-cantonal and inter-cantonal consultation and co-operation is very extensive in Switzerland. No formal federal-cantonal council has been created, but given the existence of 26 cantons, a body for their co-ordination has been considered desirable. The Conference of Cantonal Governments is intended both to facilitate inter-cantonal collaboration and, equally important, to serve as the primary channel for cantonal co-ordination in federal-cantonal consultation and negotiation.

In Belgium the federal state, the Communities, and the Regions may conclude cooperation agreements calling in particular for the joint creation and management of common services or institutions, for the joint exercise of their powers, or for the development of joint initiatives. It is left to the federation and the federated entities to undertake to create and develop these agreements, under the rules establishing their respective areas of responsibility; and they are in this sense "optional." Besides these agreements, the special law provides for a range of matters – such as so-called "mixed" international treaties – where a cooperation agreement must be signed ("obligatory" cooperation agreements).

Resolution of the many conflicts over areas of responsibility are, in principle, under the jurisdiction of the constitutional court (Cour d'arbitrage /Arbitragehof). Such a dispute may arise through right of action (at the request of the government, of a parliament, or directly of a citizen who proves to have an interest), or by exception (an interlocutory question posed by a trial judge during a proceeding). A number of criteria for the attribution of powers have therefore been established by the Court's jurisprudence. When it is called into question whether an administrative act falls within its author's areas of responsibility, the dispute falls within the jurisdiction of the Council of state, to which it is referred by right of action, or else within that of ordinary tribunals. In many cases, however, the tensions end in a compromise between levels of government. Since there are politically symmetrical coalition governments on several levels, they are probably less inclined to initiate legal disputes, and prefer to settle certain more legally delicate questions by agreements (such as cooperation agreements), as the process is simpler and there is less call for legal intervention. It is also more difficult for citizens to prove that they have an interest in disputes over areas of responsibility than in disputes over rights and freedoms.

The Belgian Coordinating Committee, a veritable intergovernmental discussion forum, serves as a space for meeting and exchange between the representatives of the different levels of government. It has been the scene of the discussion and conclusion of many agreements both formal and informal. The specialized subgroups of this committee bring together the ministers involved with certain specific portfolios (inter-ministerial committees on external relations, agriculture, etc.). There is organic cooperation (in the Coordinating Committee, for example), procedural cooperation (by assent, consultation, information procedures, etc.), and conventional cooperation. The exclusiveness of jurisdictions has not ruled out dialogue and cooperation between the different levels of government. On the contrary, owing to the interdependence between the powers of the different levels of government, cooperation has been a necessary consequence. Furthermore, it has taken diverse forms, whether informal contacts between members of government, protocols on the order of gentlemen's agreements, or full cooperation agreements.

The position of the states under the Indian Constitution can be summed up as follows:

The Constitution does not grant to any state the right of secession. The states do not have any a priori rights, but only such rights as have been expressly granted to them by the Constitution. Even the residuary rights vest in the Union Government. In the concurrent field of powers it is the Union law which prevails over a state law in the event of a conflict between the two. There is a single Constitution both for the Union and the states. There is a single unified Judiciary for the whole country and an integrated Civil Service under the supervision and control of the All Indian Services. There is a single Citizenship for the people of the country and no separate Citizenship for the people of any state. The Governors of states are appointees of the Union Government and besides being the constitutional head of the state are also the eyes and ears of the Union in the state. The Constitution guarantees individual rights and rights of certain groups, such as scheduled castes, scheduled tribes, and minorities, but not of states as such. It does not concede even the right of equal representation to the states in the Upper House of the Union Parliament.

The executive power of the Union extends to giving of such directions to a state as may appear to be necessary for that purpose. However, this does not empower the Union to interfere in any matter pertaining to the exclusive concern of a state. The Union can issue a direction only where some action of a state government is likely to prejudice the exercise of the executive power of the Union.

Union-state cooperation, as worded in Part XI of the Constitution, leaves ample scope for conflict over interpretation of definitional phrases such as "national interest" and "Union's direction." Article 263, therefore, allows the President to establish an Inter-state Council to work out modalities for continuing cooperation and to forge procedures for coordination between the Union and the states as well as among the states themselves. The text of Article 263 is so phrased as to allow the Council to discuss, debate, and recommend suitable policy measures on any subject, whether characterised as "national" or as "public." There is scope for enlarging the ambit of the council, as it would be lawful for a presidential order "to define the nature of the duties to be performed by it and its organisation and procedure." As an advisory body, the council may inquire into disputes that "have arisen between states"; investigate and discuss subjects "in which some or all of the states, or the Union and one or more of the states, have a common interest"; or recommend better coordination of policy and action on any subject necessitating interaction between the Union and the states.

There are both formal institutional and informal political arrangements for Centre-State coordination. Among the formal mechanisms are the Planning Commission, Finance Commission, National Development Council, Inter-state Council, National Integration Council, Zonal Councils, tribunals for adjudicating specific disputes, and various commissions and committees to look into specific aspects of Union-state relations. The informal mechanisms include ministerial and departmental meetings, conferences of constitutional functionaries and of political executives, and the governors' and chief ministers' conferences that are convened by the President and the Prime Minister. These informal arrangements are aimed at laying down procedural norms of conduct, particularly over such issues as the sharing of central taxes and the Union's intervention in states' affairs, and at evolving a common policy on such trans-governmental issues as the environment, communications, and health. Similarly, such informal mechanisms evolve conventions of governance on questions of states' rights, interstate trade and commerce, sharing of river waters, interstate communications, and other matters.

What is now called competition in India's negotiated federalism actually developed as a result of the emergence of coalition politics and power sharing. In this way, the Union and the states under the impact of competitive party politics and increasing regionalism have become more like coordinate centres of power. Howsoever strong the position of the Union in planning, programming, and financing, the execution of plans and projects rests in the hands of the state governments. No other large federal government is as dependent as India's on theoretically subordinate, but actually rather distinct, units responsible to a different order of government for so much of the administration of what are recognised as national programs. In the final analysis, the authority organically exercised in New Delhi is influence rather than power.

The starting point has to be adding to the competence of the Inter State Council (ISC). Since the ISC is an advisory body, it is difficult to assess the efficacy of its policy performance. And, for the same reason, its cost-effectiveness also cannot be determined. A solid institutional structure for inter-governmental cooperation has not emerged. In its functioning it has remained only an adjunct, an annexe, of the Ministry of Home Affairs. Even after its establishment, the ISC has not been able to attract sufficient attention from the state governments. With the Central government becoming weak different political parties ruling at the Union and in several states, and the Central government enjoying the majority support in the Parliament without any party being in majority..... and due to exigencies of coalition politics, the Central governments had to share power. The bargaining power of the states with the Union has markedly increased and they no longer need a mechanism like the ISC to bargain with the Union.

Accordingly, the ISC needs to be included in the process of central legislation over matters in state list. In such cases, not only informal consultations between the Union and the states should be there, but also the central government should place the proposal before the ISC before such a legislation is introduced.

The jurisdictional competence of the ISC needs to be extended so as to enable it to review every bill of national importance or which is likely to affect the interests of one or more states before it is introduced in the Parliament or a state Assembly. There should be no limitation on the ISC that it can consider only political issues.

The Union's directions to a state government, under any of the Articles, ought be issued in consultation with, and with the approval of, the Inter-state Council. Since the purpose of the setting up of the ISC was to facilitate the Union in its coordination activities, it cannot discharge its function without being a body for securing cooperation between two levels of government as well.

In this connection, the earlier recommendations of the Sarkaria Commission need a fresh review. As per the recommendations of the Sarkaria Commission, the National Development Council (NDC) and the Zonal Councils were to supplement the Inter-Governmental Council (IGC). The NDC was to be known as the National Economic And Development Council (NEDC) and the IGC would perform functions as laid down in Art.263. Thus, both the two bodies, under the chairmanship of the Prime Minister, would be performing distinct functions—the NEDC dealing with matters of socio-economic planning and development, and the IGC the remaining functions in the inter-state relations. While the Zonal Councils were to act independently of the IGC, the latter was to be a standing consultative body to review parliamentary legislation affecting the states. However, the Zonal Councils were to provide the first level of discussions on inter-state issues, and the IGC would select matters of national importance and of common interest. The Sarkaria Commission had envisioned an advisory role for the IGC and yet had believed that the Council would build mutual trust and confidence, emerging as the major instrument for discussing policies affecting inter-governmental relations. This was an optimism that was not in consonance with existing political realities. The time has come to stop believing that only the NDC represents the interests of the whole nation in planning and, therefore, an ISC cannot serve any useful purpose.

Most of the inter-governmental tensions and conflict emerge over fiscal issues, though there are constitutional mechanisms provided for such contingencies. However, the constitutional arrangements have not been objectively operated upon and, instead, the financial transfers have been politicised. In view of this, it would be worthwhile to consider a mechanism for recommending fiscal transfers by some independent body working under the auspices of the ISC. The latter needs to determine the quantum of central assistance to states and its inter-state distribution. In view of the fact that over 60 per cent of resource transfers from the Union to the states are made through the Planning Commission and the Central government's ministries, and not via the Finance Commission (which is an statutory body), it is hardly surprising that the Union's intervention in the states' development programmes has so much increased It needs to be pointed out that issues of economic planning and development cannot be settled through institutions set up be the Union government, such as

Planning and Finance Commissions. They require coordinated efforts and for that cooperated federal arrangements are needed, which role can best be provided by concerted ventures of National Development Council and the Inter state Council. The possibility of the Inter-state Council and the National Development Council merging into a common inter-governmental forum deserves serious consideration by constitutional experts and policy-makers.

In conclusion, it may be pointed out that instruments of inter-governmental cooperation have not been successful and effective because the required decentralization has not been made. This is mainly due to India's administrative centralization and earlier central planning structures. A mechanism for inter-governmental cooperation can succeed if it does not have to depend on other executive organizations for getting its decisions implemented. In the debates on federalism, special attention needs to be given—but often is not given—to the importance of inter-governmental relations and mechanisms for resolving contentious issues between different tiers of government. Inter-governmental agencies have generally operated outside the framework of the Constitution. At least in India, the inter-governmental agencies have not acquired the functional relevance visualized in the Constitution. The recommendations of inter-governmental agencies, in India, have lacked any force and have not been in a position to cope with the inter-jurisdictional strains of the Indian federal set-up. This is due to the ad hoc style of their functioning and this has eroded their credibility. Cooperative federalism can succeed only if a fair balance is maintained between the claims of diversity and the requirements of unity. If that is absent, whatever mechanisms of inter-governmental relations are devised would remain non-functional and ineffective.

The Indian Constitution would seem, in the end, to create a "cooperative union" of states rather than a dual polity. What is being observed now is federal restructuring through politically developed rules and conventions, without disturbing the basic scheme of the Constitution. The actual working of cooperative federalism in India has entailed the Union's exercising its influence rather than its constitutional authority. Exigencies of coalition politics have forced the Union and state governments to share power. The Union has more often played the role of a facilitator in interstate disputes than that of an arbitrator. A redistribution of powers—through decentralisation and the devolution of authority from the Union to the states and from the states to the panchayats and municipalities—is serving to facilitate the attainment of the objectives of the Constitution: unity, social justice, and democracy.

Further Readings

Burges, Michael and Alain-G, Gagnon, (eds.), *Comparative Federalism and Federation: Competing Trends and Future Directions*, (Hemel Hempstead: Harvester Wheatsheaf, 1993).

De Villiers, Bertus, (ed.), *Evaluating Federal Systems*, (Cape Town: Jutta & Co., 1994).

Elazar, Daniel J., (ed.), *Federal Systems of the World: A Handbook of Federal, Confederal and Autonomy Arrangements*, 2nd ed., (Harlow: Longman Group Limited, 1994).

Elaigwu, J. Isawa, *Foundations of Nigerian Federalism 1960-1995*, (Abuja: NCIR, 1996)

Franks, C.E.S., *Parliament, Intergovernmental Relations, and National Unity*, (Kingston, Queen's University: Institute for Intergovernmental Relations, 1999).

Galligan, Brian, *A Federal Republic: Australia's Constitutional System of Government*, (Oakleigh, Melbourne: Cambridge University Press, 1995).

Jeffery, C., (ed.), *Recasting German Federalism,* (London and New York: Pinter, 1999).

Majeed, Akhtar, *Federalism Within the Union,* (New Delhi: Manak, 2004).

Simeon, Richard (ed.), *Intergovernmental Relations,* (Toronto: University of Toronto Press, 1985).

Verney, Douglas V., *Federalism, Federative Systems, and Federations: The United States,* Canada and India, *Publius: The Journal of Federalism,* 25:2 (1995): 81-97.

Watts, R.L., *Comparing Federal Systems,* (Montreal and Kingston: McGill-Queen's University Press, 1966).

9

India: A Model of Cooperative Federalism

Generally, most of the federations, whether dualist or integrative in their underlying design, provide for some form of accommodative governance, sharing of institutions and some forms of joint action. A dimension that needs to be discussed is the various different ways in India in which institutions and tiers of government work with each other and with others across jurisdictional boundaries, interaction to manage inter-jurisdictional conflict and tension, the techniques and structures of interaction, and accountability and transparency. The actual operation of the Indian federation should be categorized not in terms of rigid structures for the division of powers, but as involving a process that enables reconciliation of internal diversity within the federal framework. Power-sharing, cooperation and accommodation are more effective, cheaper and lasting methods of accommodation for the developing plural societies, like the Indian. They become a meeting point for antagonistic groups and seemingly irreconcilable positions.

Comparing any two or more federal systems, we need to look at how power is divided at the centre between the executive and legislative branches, and in terms of area, i.e. between federal, state and municipal levels. There are many reasons why co-ordination is sought. Often, it is useful because programs in different jurisdictions impinge on each other. The system of the division of powers, in the governing structure, depends upon the values that are to be maximised.

Thus, the United States' governmental structure is characterised by checks and balances In the US, with the value preference for maximising the freedom of the individual there is a strict division of power at the Centre between the executive (the President) and the legislature (Congress). In terms of an area or geographic division of power, freedom against the constraint of powerful Central government was meant to be assured through "states rights" as a countervailing force against the federal government. The textbook description of American government structure has been "separation of institutions but shared powers." But the way the national government of the United States has found to try to exert its authority is through fiscal relationships, another method is legal decisions, and often both.

Nowhere does the US Constitution mention local governments, and its legal structure of federalism is "dual," with the States on one end and the nation on the other. The local governments were and remain "creatures of the states. In practice, local governments in the US are given importance because of a tradition and philosophy even if they are not "constitutionally" created at the national level, and their legal basis is clearly the state. This is based on the philosophy that any unit whose citizens elect its decision making officials, and gives them authority to enact taxes on those citizens to support it, is a government, whether it is the nation, the states, or the local governments created by the States. Often the county level of government is utilized by states to deliver services as an administrative unit, but the county is also considered a government itself. Efforts in the United States to get local governments to consolidate have mostly failed because of local citizen opposition, with a few notable exceptions where counties and cities have merged. On the other hand, the ability to create highly specific "special districts," which focus on one function such as a utility or capital intensive improvement, has resulted in the expansion of that type of government unit.

In Canada, on the other hand, the value- emphasis is on the maximisation of the welfare or results side. At the centre, in Canada, there is little division of power between the executive (Prime Minister) and the legislature (Parliament). Indeed, under this parliamentary system, the PM's control over his caucus, and hence the legislature, is legendary. In fact, the Senate is appointed, virtually for life, by the Prime Minister. Thus, Canada is a federation not by choice, but by necessity. Over decades, the combination of the political power of the provinces, and a string of constitutional court decisions interpreting provincial powers more broadly, has led to a Canada where power is not concentrated at the centre, but is shared more evenly between the provinces and the federal government. The assertiveness of the provinces has led to a federalism that is a collaboration between the provinces and the federal government. The debate in Canada is today less about division of powers and more about recognition of roles and responsibilities.

In Switzerland, the underlying philosophy is that, in order to establish and limit political power, federal constituents must have legitimacy of the great majority of the concerned cultural communities; and this legitimacy can be achieved if the different communities have the power to participate on equal footing in the constitution-making process. Article 2 of the Constitution mandates the Confederation to enhance and promote the cultural diversity. In this way, the federal government gets additional powers and responsibilities, as against the traditional Cantonal competences, in the fields of culture, religion and education. No doubt, Cantons are sovereign in matters of their culture and linguistic policy but these policies have to conform to the limitations of Article 70 wherein the Confederation has the additional responsibility to encourage the understanding among different linguistic communities. According to Article 52 (1) of the Swiss Constitution the Confederation shall protect the constitutional order of the cantons. While primary responsibility for ensuring constitutional order lies with the cantons (Article 57 of the Constitution), the Confederation and the other cantons are called to support the concerned canton if it cannot ensure its own constitutional order (*principle of comity*). This duty of support is based on Article 44 (1)-(2) of the Constitution, which states that the Confederation and the cantons shall support each other in the fulfillment of their tasks. A federal intervention is foreseen when the inner order of a canton is disturbed or threatened and cannot be protected by the canton alone or with the help of other cantons (Article 52 (2) of the Constitution).

The 1999 Swiss Constitution places more emphasis on the principle of cooperation than on the principle of self-rule as expressed by the autonomy of the Cantons. This Constitution has introduced three major changes : I – the right of the Cantons to participate in the foreign policy decisions of the federal government, 2 – the general right to participate in internal federal legislation, and 3 – the general possibility for Cantons to regulate matters of general concern through inter-cantonal or international treaties. In order to participate in the federal decision-making processes, Cantonal executives created a new body—Council of Presidents of Cantonal Governments—and this has enabled the Cantons to use new ways and means for inter-cantonal partnership and cooperation.

The German federation is the best example of being moulded on cooperative lines. The horizontal division of power, which tends to characterise that system leaves most principal questions of policy to the federation. The states (*Lander*) actively participate in the federal decision making process through their participation in the federal council (*Bundesrat*). Most administration constitutionally is assigned to the sphere of the Lander, through the federal and state bureaucracies that duplicate each other. The court hierarchy reflects these arrangements, providing a single avenue for the resolution of disputes irrespective of the jurisdiction in which they arise.

There are three *levels* of intergovernmental mechanisms in Germany and their main functions are:

— co-ordination and preparation of voting, and finally voting itself about federal and European legislation at the level of the "federal state."
— mutual consultation and co-operation in all fields and in particular in overlapping areas of competence at the level of the "Whole state," and
— co-ordination in the preparation of both Länder and federal legislation as also (and sometimes primarily) on matters of administration on the Third Level.

The entire intergovernmental structure in Germany is

governed by the overarching principle of *federal comity* or *loyalty (Bundestreue)*, which permeates all institutional and behavioural emanations of federal practice. It focuses on the demand that both the Federation and the Lander have to take care of "mutual considerateness" in the exercise of their respective powers and that all of their actions and intentions must be "friendly to the idea of federation."

Throughout the 90s, in Brazil, a decentralisation of responsibilities in social policies took place. The concentration of authority in the federal government characterises federal relations in policy management, because the Union exercises the role of main funding agent, and of regulator and co-ordinator of intergovernmental relations. As a general rule, a direct relationship has been established between federal government and municipalities. under which the latter operate as service executors. This design arose in great part from an effort to match the tax decentralisation of the 80s with responsibility for provision of social services.

A country the size of a continent, with an area of 12,65 000 sq. miles and the population of over a Billion, India is the most extreme plural society with 22 national languages and some 2000 dialects, a dozen ethnic and seven religious groups fragmented into a large number of sects, castes and sub-castes, and some sixty socio-cultural sub-regions spread over seven natural geographic regions. Existence of such identities, and such perceptions, cannot be wished away. A viable and successful polity must recognize these identities, respect them and must accommodate them. The Constitution of India has done just that and, in this way, through the assurance of providing Good / Quality Governance, and cooperative federalism, has become the best guarantee for a viable and vibrant nation. In multi-cultural, multi-ethnic and plural societies, like in India, and many others, social justice, economic progress and political democracy can be achieved only through an accommodation of diverse interests and identities.

As the society in India is plural, whereas the nation-state is uniform and polity is federal, potentialities of strife and frictions are all too obvious The guarantee for the sustenance of a plural society has been provided by the Constitution of India in a self-equilibrating system, which does not allow one group or one party or one interest any enduring dominance. The Constitution describes India 'a Union of States' and this implies the indestructible nature of its unity (Ref. Preamble to the Constitution of India). The Indian system does not treat plural diversity as a threat to integration for the nation, though in some countries it has become a fertile ground for the same as the political system was not accommodative enough to let the articulation of diversities manifest. In India, the desire to identify some common goals and purposes, and to establish not just political legitimacy but political accountability, has become the basis of nationhood. If power is properly shared and varied interests are accommodated, there need not be any threat to power. The Indian federal mechanism is intended to provide precisely the same. In the above context, the Indian federal Union was formed by reconciling various visions, diversities, ideologies and influences. The federal Union was formed with some basic objectives to (i) put in place a mechanism of federal governance with a strong parliamentary centre, (ii) guarantee cultural autonomy to regions with strong linguistic, religious, tribal, and/or territorial identities, (iii) create a mixed economy with sectors demarcated for state and private enterprise, and (iv) reduce regional and economic disparities through fiscal federalism and planning. As the Indian constitutional structure has shown, it is possible to respect cultural diversity without having to fear a wrecking of the nation-state. Ultimately, it is not just the question of majority-minority in a plural society; it is the question of social and distributive justice in a liberal democracy. If democracy is not receptive to various identities in a plural society then it remains only a majoritarian democracy that 'disprivileges' the minorities. The viable alternative is that which has been provided under the Constitution of India (Ref. Articles 25 to 30 of the Constitution of India). Since the democratic procedures and institutions, in the normal course, would work in a manner that would be disadvantageous to the minorities, the state has ensured special provisions for the protection of minority rights.

Recognition of minority rights in the Constitution of India is important in this context. This does not mean any conflict between the group rights of minorities and individual rights. Nevertheless, some sort of groups rights have to be reorganized, compatible with individual rights and that would be a combination of multi-layered federalism, democracy compatible with federalism, acceptance of multiculturalism and acceptance of minority rights compatible with individual rights. That is the way of assuaging apprehensions regarding cultural identities in a federal democracy. That is the way of governing in the form of a 'cooperative federalism,' given the hierarchical social order that exists in India. The primary purpose of democratic procedures is not the rule of the majority but a shared-rule by achieving the widest possible consensus. When the decision-making processes are decentralized, the result is a consensual democracy which is much more stable in societies that are multi-ethnic, multi-cultural and are diverse, like the Indian.

Before independence, the sub-nationalist identities were not even adequately realized. It was much later on that it was realized that federalism could be a good device for solving the problems based on ethnicity, language and others if these ethnicities are territorially identifiable.

In India, the federal constituents are states, which are 'unit of self rule,' through which autonomy of the society (in terms of maintenance of identity and assured development) gets operationalized. People having distinct socio-cultural identity, concentrated in few contiguous districts within the existing state-systems, sought a separate state in order to preserve, protect and promote their identity. They believed that a separate state would provide them a political identity and a constitutionally documented institutional space for interest articulation and protection within the broader territorial state. In India, the unit of self rule may be: (i) a full-fledged state; (ii) autonomous region or regional councils with adequate legislative and executive powers within the existing states in which they are included; (iii) district development council with adequate authority over local planning for the people located in 'ethnic enclaves' of an otherwise composite state; and (iv) granting of Union Territory status to city regions, strategically important region or sub-region and to those areas which are extremely backward Governed directly by the Union Government, Union Territories were created for small areas having special cultural heritage or for an area coming under the inter-state dispute. Statehood may be granted to those regional communities which do qualify the three-point criteria of: (i) administrative and political manageability involving closer contact between the people and their elected representatives; (ii) techno-economic viability; and (iii) socio-cultural homogeneity (in terms of tribes\jatis, language\dialect, belief system\religious communities and ethnic identities). In order to promote federal stability at the macro level, the institutions of shared rule such as Zonal Councils, Inter-state Councils, etc., were activated. These institutions are advisory or recommendatory bodies, facilitating inter-state cooperation and coordination in the areas of national and regional planning and development.

Arguments in favor of the formation or reorganization of states, among others, have been geographical proximity, a common language, similar usages and customs, comparable socio-economic and political stages of development, common historical traditions and experiences, a common way of living, administrative expediency, and, more than anything else, a widely prevalent sentiment of "togetherness", that is, a sense of identity (Rasheeduddin Khan, 1992, 109). In the competition for resources, the regions used several benchmarks to establish their identity. They were language, culture, economic advancement, administrative coherence, and even the socio-economic backwardness of the region (due to its being part of a bigger regional unit). Regional movements sparked demands for the formation of new states, and for the reorganization of existing states. These demands did not usually go beyond claiming resource-sharing within the broader national context. In this, language was often the symbol giving expression to these aspirations. A close scrutiny of state-formation in India would reveal that, together with languages, many variable and critical factors like ethnic-cum-economic consideration (Nagaland, Meghalaya, Manipur and Tripura); religion, script and sentiments (Haryana and Punjab); language-cum-culture (Maharashtra and Gujarat); historical and political factors (Uttar Pradesh and Bihar); integration of Princely states and the need for viable groupings (Madhya Pradesh and Rajasthan) and of course, language-cum-social distinctiveness (Tamilnadu, Kerala, Mysore, Andhra Pradesh, Assam, Bengal and

Orissa) have played a decisive role in the composition of the Indian federation. A successful working of India's federal nation would involve administrative sub-division of larger states on the principles of regional autonomy and regional identity. The large composite states face problems of governance, and their very size may hamper economic development. Today's Uttar Pradesh, Bihar, Madhya Pradesh, and Rajasthan provide examples of states with problems. When the people are made partners in governance, the nation as such is strengthened. Comparable development is possible elsewhere with the decentralization of power, and may lessen the demands for separate states. One should not rush to assume that granting more administrative and fiscal powers to the states, or creating a large number of states, may weaken the country.

States need to be reorganized in a manner which may accommodate and institutionalize various sub-regional identities. One way could be to identify a four-variables' basis for re-organization: administrative convenience, economic viability, similarity in the developmental needs of a sub-region, and cultural-linguistic affinity. On this basis, even if more states are formed, it would only be strengthening the self-rule, shared-rule principle of cooperative federalism. And that would provide quality governance, as well.

In view of historical traditions of centralization of power and authority, the operative principle in the making of India's Constitution was that a government was best when it was able to bring about social transformation. Hence, the framers of the Constitution and the subsequent law-makers consciously ensured that the overwhelming majority of powers and authority was kept with the union government, with the result that there is "blood pressure at the Centre and anemia at the periphery," resulting in morbidity and inefficiency. Equally important, the country's diversity and socio-economic conditions, coupled with the ideological influences of socialism, drove the Constitution toward a kind of organically unitary federalism in the name of justice, equality, and rights protection

However, the wide powers given to the Union, and limited powers given to the states must not be seen in terms of either-or-federalism of the past, which rested on a dichotomy between the Union and the states (Akhtar Majeed, 2005, 74). The two should not be seen as competing centers of power but as co-partners in the task of nation building. The Union has been assigned the duty of nation-building, maintenance of unity, protection of territorial integrity of the country and maintenance of constitutional-political order throughout the country. The states are to cooperate with the Union in the performance of these functions and in discharging their own constitutional duties with regard to subjects that are local. But as soon as any subject ceases to be 'local,' the Union would intervene to legislate on that subject.

The Indian Constitution would seem, in the end, to create a cooperative union of states rather than a dual polity What is being observed now is federal restructuring through politically developed rules and conventions, without disturbing the basic scheme of the Constitution. The actual working of cooperative federalism in India has entailed the Union's exercising its influence rather than its constitutional authority. Exigencies of coalition politics have forced the Union and state governments to share power. The Union has more often played the role of a facilitator in interstate disputes than that of an arbitrator. A redistribution of powers – through decentralisation and the devolution of authority from the Union to the states and from the states to the local bodies and municipalities – is serving to facilitate the attainment of the objectives of the Constitution: unity, social justice, and democracy. System is a device of shared-governance, and the Constitution of India envisages a 'creative balance' between the need for an effective Union and effectively – empowered states· There is a paradigm shift from the principle of dual- federalism (with each tier of government exercising its own powers) to cooperative-federalism (with the federal and state governments interacting with each other in the formulation and implementation of public policy). India is one such example of cooperative federalism with variations in the degree in which policy-areas are handled by different tiers of government. Overall, the impression is that inter-governmental relations in India focus more on the needs of the citizens—particularly in welfare policy areas—rather than on questions of turf and jurisdiction.

For power sharing a sense of accommodation is to be there, and a paradigm shift is needed in which democracy need not be just representative but a participatory democracy, and that is the direction towards which Indian federalism is now moving. In the constitutional scheme of distribution of responsibilities, the persistent theme revolves around cooperative federalism. If the lower/sub-federal level (*Panchayats*, urban local governments) depend on the higher levels of government, for money and resources, the latter (Union and state governments, both) depend on the former for providing services to the people.

The practical importance of the Concurrent list, (when adopted in any federation) lies in the fact, that the vesting of the same type of power in two parallel agencies carries, within it, the seeds of a possible conflict. This implies, that the Constitution should provide, in advance, a mechanism for resolving such conflict. In India, Constitution primarily seeks to incorporate such a mechanism. (a) The co-existence of Union and state laws in a particular area can give rise to litigation. Such problems arise, either because the Union or a state may illegally encroach upon the province of the other (parallel) legislature, or they may arise because (though there is no encroachment, as such, on each other's sphere), the two laws clash with each other. (b) The two situations are, strictly speaking, different from each other; and in India they are judged by two different tests. Where the subject-matter of the legislation in question falls within either the Union List or the State List only, then the question is decided with reference to legislative competence. One of the two laws must necessarily be void, because (leaving aside matters in the Concurrent List), the Indian Constitution confers exclusive jurisdiction upon Parliament for matters in the Union List and upon a state Legislature for matters in the state List. The Union is not empowered to interfere in any matter pertaining to the exclusive concern of a state. The correct doctrine applicable in such cases is that of ultra vires. Since one of the two laws must be void, the question of inconsistency between the two has no relevance. Only one law will survive; and the other law will not survive, because ex-hypothesis, it has no life. (c) In contrast, where the legislation passed by the Union and the state is on a subject matter included in the Concurrent List, then the matter is not determined by applying the test of ultra vires because the hypothesis is that both the laws are (apart from repugnancy), constitutionally valid. In such a case, in the Constitution of India, the test to be adopted is that of repugnancy.

It is obvious, that where either the Union or the state legislature proposes to enact a law, it must, in the first place, decide whether it has legislative competence with reference to the subject matter of the law.

Sharing among regions is not unique to federations.

What makes the Indian federation different is not the fact of interregional redistribution *per se*, but the fact that it is explicit (Vithal and Sastry, 2001, 255). Indeed, the analog between interregional sharing within a federation and that within a unitary state in part accounts for the use of the financial arrangements of the unitary state as a benchmark for judging interregional sharing in a federation.

Interregional fiscal sharing schemes take different forms in different federations, depending especially on the nature and extent of the fiscal responsibilities assumed by the regions. Unlike the indian one, regions in such federations have significant expenditure responsibilities, but rely on the Central government for their finances. Financing can be formula-based or it can have significant discretionary elements in it. In India, intergovernmental fiscal sharing schemes essentially complement policies implemented by the various levels of government and apply intact regardless of the extent of vertical redistribution pursued by governments. They can be looked at as policies that facilitate the decentralization of fiscal responsibilities, ensuring that the benefits of decentralization are achieved without compromising national objectives of efficiency and equity.

An important feature of India's Fiscal Federalism is revenue sharing between the Union and the states. Finally, Parliament is empowered to make such grants as it deems necessary to providing financial assistance for any state in need. Such grants can be block grants or specific categorical grants. There is a clear vertical imbalance between (1) the powers of taxation assigned to the Union and the states and (2) the social and economic responsibilities assigned to the states. That is, the states' responsibilities exceed their own-source revenues. But, the Finance Commission, the Planning Commission, and the National Development Council provide mechanisms for periodically correcting this imbalance and for allowing the states to better discharge their responsibilities. These forums cater to the grievances of the states, which they redress to the extent possible.

The Constitution provides that the distribution between the Union and the states of the net proceeds of taxes that are to be divided between them, and the allocation between states of the respective shares of such proceeds, shall be done on the recommendations of a Finance Commission that is appointed by the President every five years. The Commission also recommends the principles that should govern grants-in-aid to the states. The grants are both a means to assist development schemes in states lacking adequate financial resources and an instrument to exercise control and coordination over the states' welfare schemes.

The following provisions of the Constitution are noteworthy in this connection:

(1) There are duties levied by the Union but collected and appropriated by the states.
(2) There are taxes levied and collected by the Union but assigned wholly to the states.
(3) There are taxes levied and collected by the Union and distributed between the Union and the states. This is the position of taxes on income other than agricultural income.
(4) There are taxes and duties which are levied and collected by the Union and may be distributed between the Union and the states if Parliament by law so provides.

Plan grants, provided are 50-50 matching grants, which means that the Union government issues a grant equal to the sum that the state has raised through its own resources. It also means that states have to fall in line with

Union policies, priorities, and preferences in issuing matching grants and also dovetail their own funds to Union allocations.

There is a Third-Tier of Indian federal structure, comprised of Local-governing bodies. Part IX of the Constitution outlines the framework of institutions of rural self-government: a three-tier system of units known, in ascending order, as the village, intermediate, and district *panchayats*. This system came into existence with two basic objectives: (a) democratic decentralisation and (b) local participation in planned programmes.

Part IXA of the Constitution sets forth the framework of urban local government. Three types of institutions of local self-government have been provided for urban areas, namely "*nagar panchayats*" for transitional areas (i.e., areas that are being transformed from rural to urban), municipal councils for small urban areas, and municipal corporations for large urban areas. Every state is obliged to constitute such units. Local government remains an exclusive state subject. The Constitution provides for direct election of local bodies, in urban and rural areas, every five years. The other noticeable provisions are:

(i) reservation of seats for women and for scheduled castes and tribes,

(ii) a state Finance Commission to ensure financial viability of these institutions,

(iii) devolution of powers and responsibilities to the local bodies with respect to:

   (a) preparation of plans and implementation of schemes for economic development and social justice,

   (b) devolution of financial powers to the local bodies,

   (c) endowment of these institutions with powers,

authority and responsibility to prepare plans for economic development and community welfare programmes for revenue raising responsibilities.

Panchayats and local urban bodies have now been given powers and responsibilities to plan and execute economic development programmes, social justice and the implementation of schemes listed in the Constitution. These activities include: anti-poverty programmes, such as Integrated Rural Development Programme, land improvement, minor irrigation, social forestry, small scale and cottage industry; Primary and Secondary Schools, non-formal education, technical training; health and sanitation and family welfare; social welfare, welfare of weaker sections, public distribution system and women and child development; roads, housing, drinking water, markets, electrification, maintenance of community assets etc. But the local bodies have such a limited scope for revenue generation, and relatively a vast area of jurisdiction, that they are perennially dependent upon the states for the latter's grants. The local bodies have to depend almost entirely on state governments for discharging responsibilities assigned to them. The constitutional difficulty is in the fact that devolution of powers and responsibilities for Panchayats are listed but an elaborate scheme has not been provided regarding their sources of finance. Thus, what has been rganization is the assignment of functions and not the resources. Further, because the state governments are reluctant to part with revenue-generating powers, fiscal autonomy is actually denied to the Panchayats and urban local bodies. (Anwar Shah, 2006).

In this constitutional scheme of distribution of responsibilities, the persistent theme revolves around cooperative federalism. If the Third Tier (Panchayats, and urban local governments depend on the other two tiers of government, for money and resources, the latter (Union and state governments, both) depend on the former for providing services to the people.

Cooperative federalism can succeed only if a fair balance is maintained between the claims of diversity and the requirements of unity. If that is absent, whatever mechanisms of inter-governmental relations are devised would remain non-functional and ineffective. The constitutional provisions stipulate that the state shall decide about the resource-transfers to local bodies. Any transfer mechanism increases the dependence of the local level units. Local units are expected to collect taxes because they are self-governing units, but the system works on the principle of "you collect and I will transfer". But the cordial principle of governance is that the government should meet its expenditure or, at least, revenue on core services should come from its own resources. This should be by right and not through benevolence of any other government. What needs to be transferred is a power to collect resources, to garner resources, and the power to tax. Unless that is there, local units remain locally dependent units, not local self-governing units.

Decentralised and grass-root planning and implementation are features of shared governance; and this, in turn, reflects the correct image of federal governance. Social federalism cannot be sidelined in the name of political federalism. Local bodies in India function more closely with community-based organisations, with the user-groups or stakeholders in development. The starting point is not just distribution of functions but transferring functions to these bodies and allocating funds to them, thus making them competent to perform the functions constitutionally assigned to them

After the States Reorganisation Act 1956, five Zonal Councils were set up, each composed of the chief ministers of the states in a council's zone, the development ministers and chief secretaries of these states, and a member of the Planning Commission, with each council headed by the Union's home minister. The zonal councils are intended to foster the psychological integration of the country by mitigating regional consciousness; helping the Union and state governments to evolve uniform social and economic policies; assisting with effective implementation of development projects; and evolving a degree of political equilibrium among the regions of the country. The Autonomous District Councils (ADCs), provide in-built safeguards in the in the Constitution which maintain and strengthen the rights of the minority and micro-minority groups while empowering them with greater responsibilities and opportunities, for example, through the process of Central funding for Plan expenditure instead of routing all funds through the state Governments. They play a Central role here by developing a process of public education on the proposed changes, which would assure communities about protection of their traditions and also bring in gender representation and give voice to other ethnic groups.

Union-state cooperation, as worded in the Constitution, leaves ample scope for conflict over interpretation of definitional phrases. The Constitution, therefore, allows the President to establish an *Inter-state Council* (ISC) to work out modalities for continuing cooperation and to forge procedures for coordination between the Union and the states as well as among the states themselves. The text is so phrased as to allow the council to discuss, debate, and recommend suitable policy measures on any subject. There is scope for enlarging the ambit of the council, as it would be lawful for the Presidential order "to define the nature of the duties to be performed by it and its rganization and procedure." As an advisory body, the council may inquire into disputes that "have arisen between states"; investigate and discuss subjects "in which some or all of the states, or the Union and one or more of the states, have a common interest"; or recommend better coordination of policy and action on any subject necessitating interaction between the Union and the states. For smooth running of federal relations, the starting point has to be adding to the competence of the Inter state Council (ISC). Since the ISC is an advisory body, it is difficult to assess the efficacy of its policy performance. And, for the same reason, its cost-effectiveness also cannot be determined. A solid institutional structure for inter-governmental cooperation has not emerged. The ISC needs to be included in the process of central legislation over matters in state list. In such cases, not only informal consultations between the Union and the states should be there, but also the central government should place the proposal before the ISC before such a legislation is introduced. The jurisdictional competence of the ISC needs to be extended so as to enable it to review every bill of national importance or which is likely to affect the interests of one or more states before it is introduced in the Parliament or a state Assembly. There should be no limitation on the ISC that it can consider only political issues. The Union's directions to a state government, under any of the Articles, ought to be issued in consultation with, and with the approval of, the Inter-state Council. Since the purpose of the setting up of the ISC was to facilitate the Union in its coordination activities, it cannot discharge its function without being a body for securing cooperation between two levels of government as well.

Because the Union grants are routed through central ministries to their counterparts in the states, each Union ministry is in a position to use the strings of financial power to superintend, direct, and control the corresponding state department. In this way, besides the territorial or horizontal federation set up by the Constitution, a sort of vertical federation has come into being. Yet, there is kind of subsidiary element in different units of the constituent federal system. The mechanism of inter-governmental relations in India are tilted in favour of the Union government. There are inter-governmental institutions meant to exercise some uniformity in administrative relations. The hegemony or the dominance of the Union governmental institutions over the state governments is meant to bring about some kind of uniformity of standards in administrative procedures. In some respects, states have also acquired certain say in matters which used to be traditionally the domain of the Union. One reason is the regional parties sharing political power at the Union. In terms of foreign affairs, states that have economically performed well, and have attracted Foreign Direct Investment, have influenced the foreign economic policy of the Union. States are now more conscious of their role in foreign affairs with neighbouring countries as well as international organizations like WTO, World Bank, ADB etc. Thus, inter-governmental relations reflect both the tendencies of conflict and cooperation, and they keep changing.

There are both formal institutional and informal political arrangements for union-state coordination. Among the formal mechanisms are the Planning Commission, Finance Commission, National Development Council, Inter-state Council, National Integration Council, zonal councils, tribunals for adjudicating specific disputes, and various commissions and committees to look into specific aspects of Union-state relations. The informal mechanisms include ministerial and departmental meetings, conferences of constitutional functionaries and of political executives, and the governors' and chief ministers' conferences that are convened by the President and the Prime Minister. These informal arrangements are aimed at laying down procedural norms of conduct, particularly over such issues as the sharing of central taxes and the Union's intervention in states' affairs, and at evolving a common policy on such trans-governmental issues as the environment, communications, and health. Similarly, such informal mechanisms evolve conventions of governance on questions of states' rights, interstate trade and commerce, sharing of river waters, interstate communications, and other matters.

Cooperative federalism, as envisaged by the Constitution, is possible when these inter-governmental institutions become effectively operative. A mechanism for inter-governmental cooperation can succeed if it does not have to depend on other executive organizations for getting its decisions implemented.. It needs to be pointed out that issues of economic planning and development cannot be settled through institutions set up be the central government, such as Planning and Finance Commissions. They require coordinated efforts and for that cooperated federal arrangements are needed, which role can best be provided by concerted ventures of National Development council and the Inter state Council.

In the debates on federalism, special attention needs to be given—but often is not given in India—to the importance of inter-governmental relations and mechanisms for resolving contentious issues between different tiers of government. Such an academic attention is particularly needed for plural societies where different socio-economic interests vie for political control of the national polity. Inter-governmental agencies have generally operated outside the framework of the Constitution. At least in India, the inter-governmental agencies have not acquired the functional relevance visualized in the Constitution. The recommendations of inter-governmental agencies, in India, have lacked any force and have not been in a position to cope with the inter-jurisdictional strains of the Indian federal set-up. This is due to the ad hoc style of their functioning and this has eroded their credibility. Cooperative federalism can succeed only if a fair balance is maintained between the claims of diversity and the requirements of unity. If that is absent, whatever mechanisms of inter-governmental relations are devised would remain non-functional and ineffective.

What is now called competition in India's negotiated/ cooperative federalism actually developed as a result of the emergence of coalition politics and power sharing. In this way, the Union and the states under the impact of competitive party politics and increasing regionalism have become more like coordinate centres of power.

In the debates over the working of the Indian federal working, one point is missed out: if any monitoring by the Union over the states—as far as funding of local bodies is concerned—is an attempt to further centralisation, so is the financial choking of the local bodies by the state governments. It is not as if federalism is in jeopardy when the Union does something that the states do not like, but federalism is safe when the states do not provide competence to the local bodies. The point that is missed is that the Union and the states are not the only constituents of our federalism; there is a third-tier also at the local level.

The debate focuses on the constitutional division of responsibilities between the Union and the states and this, supposedly, is the basis of India's federal structure. Responsibilities of various tiers of government are determined by the functions that are assigned to them. The ability and competence to perform these functions depend on the earmarking of sources of finance. Any efficient demarcation of functions and finances is possible if a cost-effective analysis is first made of the efficiency of different tiers to undertake some functions. This has to be followed by some monitoring to assess how successfully, effectively and efficiently the resources were utilised by a government. 'Process Improvement' in industrial management involves removing a few layers, and this results in speedy and effective disbursement.

By constitutional amendments, rural and urban local bodies have also been provided with specific domains of governance. The starting point has to be not just distribution of functions but transferring functions to these bodies and allocating funds to them, thus making them competent to perform the functions constitutionally assigned to them.

The Indian Constitution would seem, in the end, to create a "cooperative union" of states rather than a dual polity. What is being observed now is federal restructuring through politically developed rules and conventions, without disturbing the basic scheme of the Constitution. The actual working of cooperative federalism in India has entailed the Union's exercising its influence rather than its constitutional authority. Exigencies of coalition politics have forced the Union and state governments to share power. The Union has more often played the role of a facilitator in interstate disputes than that of an arbitrator. A redistribution of powers – through decentralisation and the devolution of authority from the Union to the states and from the states to the *panchayats* and municipalities –- is serving to facilitate the attainment of the objectives of the Constitution: unity, social justice, and democracy.

Further Readings

Basu, D.D., *Introduction to the Constitution of India* (19 edn.), (New Delhi: Wadhwa & Company, 2002); P.M. Bakshi, *The Constitution of India,* (New Delhi: Universal Law Publishing Co.: 2009); Granvile Austin, *Working a Democratic Constitution,* (New Delhi: Oxford, 1999); and A.G. Noorani, *Constitutional Questions in India,* (New Delhi: Oxford, 2000).

Khan, Rasheeduddin, *Federal India: A Design for Change,* (New Delhi: Vikas 1992).

Majeed, Akhtar, *Federalism Within the Union: Distribution of Responsibilities in the Indian System,* (New Delhi: Manak, 2005).

Majeed, Akhtar, Ronald R. Watts, Douglas M. Brown, *Distribution of Powers and Responsibilities in Federal Polities,* (Montreal: McGill Queens, 2006).

Mathur, Om Prakash, "Local Government Organization and Finance: Urban India," in Anwar Shah (ed.), *Local Governance in Developing Countries,* (Washington, DC: World Bank, 2006).

Vithal, B.P.R. and M.L. Sastry, *Fiscal Federalism in India,* (New Delhi: Oxford, 2001); and Govinda Rao and Nirvikar Singh, *Political Economy of Federalism in India,* (New Delhi: Oxford, 2005).

Vora, Rajendra and Anne Feldhaus, *Region, Culture and Politics in India,* (New Delhi: Manohar 2006); and Rob Jenkins *Regional Reflections: Comparing Politics Across India's States,* (New Delhi: Oxford, 2004).

10

Shared-Rule-Self-Rule in the Working of Indian Federalism

Writing about distribution of responsibilities in federal polities, Ronald Watts[1] maintains that the actual operation of federations should be categorized not in terms of rigid structures for the division of powers, but as involving a process that enables reconciliation of internal diversity within their federal frameworks. In a plural society, Federalism is a method of Good Governance in which political accommodation and understanding become a sound practice for governance in the midst of conflicting ideologies, disparate groups and seemingly irreconcilable positions. Power-sharing, cooperation and accommodation are more effective, cheaper and lasting methods of accommodation for the developing plural societies. They become a meeting point for antagonistic groups and seemingly irreconcilable positions. Watts has quoted the argument[2] that just as in the economic realm competition produces superior benefits compared to monopolies or oligopolies, so competition between governments serving the same citizens is likely to provide those citizens with better service.

Many authors[3] have maintained that in the post-colonial era, state in a plural and multi-cultural society continued with the colonial technique of intervention or non-intervention in the affairs of diverse social groups when it suited the ruling elite. The power of such a nation-state derived from nationalist mobilisation. In a majoritarian democracy, the national elite gets to dominate all spheres of social life, of all sections of society, all domains with an acquired legitimacy. And it is easy to charge any group with betrayal if this legitimacy is questioned. Because the 'nation' as such creates an illusion, a perception, of consensus and uniformity, there is hardly any scope for the society distinct from the state. As the society in India is plural, whereas the nation-state is uniform and polity is federal, potentialities of strife and frictions are all too obvious. The guarantee for the sustenance of a plural society has been provided by the Constitution of India in a self-equilibrating system, which does not allow one group or one party or one interest any enduring dominance. The Constitution describes India 'a Union of States' and this implies the indestructible nature of its unity. The Indian system does not treat plural diversity as a threat to integration for the nation, though in some countries it has become a fertile ground for the same as the political system was not accommodative enough to let the articulation of diversities manifest. In India, the desire to identify some common goals and purposes, and to establish not just political legitimacy but political accountability, has become the basis of nationhood. If power is properly shared and varied interests are accommodated, there need not be any threat to power. The Indian federal mechanism is intended to provide precisely the same.

In the above context, the Indian federal Union was formed by reconciling various visions, diversities, ideologies and influences. From this emerged a synthesis that became the base of Indian Constitution, the pillars being: universal adult franchise, democratic liberal-federal republicanism, secularism, universal and fundamental rights, state intervention against inherited inequalities, positive discrimination to support the disadvantaged, and social justice. The Federal Union was formed with some basic objectives to (i) put in place a mechanism of federal governance with a strong parliamentary centre, (ii) guarantee cultural autonomy to regions with strong linguistic, religious, tribal, and/or territorial identities, (iii) create a mixed economy with sectors demarcated for state and private enterprise, and (iv) reduce regional and economic disparities through fiscal federalism and planning.

The nationalist movement, before independence, was so strong that the sub-nationalist identities were not even adequately realized. It was much later on that it was realized that federalism could be a good device for solving the problems based on ethnicity, language and others if these ethnicities are territorially identifiable. In view of historical traditions of centralization of power and authority, the operative principle in the making of India's Constitution was that a government was best when it was able to bring about social transformation. Hence, the framers of the Constitution and the subsequent law-makers consciously ensured that the overwhelming majority of powers and authority was kept with the union government. Equally important, the country's diversity and socio-economic conditions, coupled with the ideological influences of socialism, drove the Constitution toward a kind of organically unitary federalism in the name of justice, equality, and rights protection

However, the two should not be seen as competing centers of power but as co-partners in the task of nation building. The Union has been assigned the duty of nation-building, maintenance of unity, protection of territorial integrity of the country and maintenance of constitutional-political order throughout the country. The states are to cooperate with the Union in the performance of these functions and in discharging their own constitutional duties with regard to subjects that are local. But as soon as any subject ceases to be 'local,' the Union would intervene to legislate on that subject.

The Indian Constitution would seem, in the end, to create a cooperative union of states rather than a dual polity. What is being observed now is federal restructuring through politically developed rules and conventions, without disturbing the basic scheme of the Constitution. The actual working of cooperative federalism in India has entailed the Union's exercising its influence rather than its constitutional authority. Exigencies of coalition politics have forced the Union and state governments to share power. The Union has more often played the role of a facilitator in interstate disputes than that of an arbitrator. A redistribution of powers —through decentralisation and the devolution of authority from the Union to the states and from the states to the local bodies and municipalities—is serving to facilitate the attainment of the objectives of the Constitution: unity, social justice, and democracy. Any federal system is a device of shared-governance, and the Constitution of India envisages a 'creative balance' between the need for an effective Union and effectively-empowered states.[4] A healthy sign is the growing realisation that inter-governmental relations need to focus more on the needs of the citizens—particularly in welfare policy areas—rather than on questions of turf and jurisdiction. For power sharing a sense of accommodation is to be there, and a paradigm shift is needed in which democracy need not be just representative but a participatory democracy, and that is the direction towards which Indian federalism is now moving.

In India, Article 254 of the Constitution primarily seeks to incorporate such a mechanism.

(a) The co-existence of Central and state laws in a particular area can give rise to litigation. Such problems arise, either because the Union or a state may illegally encroach upon the province of the other (parallel) legislature, or they may arise because (though there is no encroachment, as such, on each other's sphere), the two laws clash with each other.

(b) The two situations are, strictly speaking, different from each other; and they must be judged by two different tests. Where the subject-matter of the legislation in question falls within either the Union List or the state list only, then the question is to be decided with reference to legislative competence. One of the two laws must necessarily be void, because (leaving aside matters in the Concurrent List), the Indian Constitution confers exclusive jurisdiction upon Parliament for matters in the Union List and upon a state Legislature for matters in the state List. The Union is not empowered to interfere in any matter pertaining to the exclusive concern of a State[5]. The correct doctrine applicable in such cases is that of ultra vires. Since one of the two laws must be void, the question of inconsistency between the two has no relevance. Only one law will survive; and the other law will not survive, because ex hypothesi, it has no life.

(c) In contrast, where the legislation passed by the

> Union and the state is on a subject matter included in the Concurrent List, then the matter cannot be determined by applying the test of ultra vires because the hypothesis is, that both the laws are (apart from repugnancy), constitutionally valid. In such a case, the test to be adopted will be that of repugnancy, under article 254(2), of the Constitution.

It is obvious, that where either the Union or the state legislature proposes to enact a law, it must, in the first place, decide whether it has legislative competence with reference to the subject matter of the law.

Sharing among regions is not unique to federations. In unitary states, it occurs virtually automatically and with little fanfare. Unitary state governments typically design tax systems on a nation-wide basis such that persons in like circumstance are treated comparably regardless of where they reside. And, public services are usually provided at uniform levels to individuals everywhere in the nation. The consequence is that there is considerable implicit redistribution from high-income to low-income regions. By the same token, within regions, persons in different localities are treated comparably, implying possibly significant implicit intra-regional redistribution. What makes a federation different is not the fact of interregional redistribution per se, but the fact that it is explicit. Indeed, the analog between interregional sharing within a federation and that within a unitary state in part accounts for the use of the financial arrangements of the unitary state as a benchmark for judging interregional sharing in a federation. Interregional fiscal sharing schemes take different forms in different federations, depending especially on the nature and extent of the fiscal responsibilities assumed by the regions. In some federations, regions have significant expenditure responsibilities, but rely on the central government for their finances. Financing can be formula-based or it can have significant discretionary elements in it.

Intergovernmental fiscal sharing schemes essentially complement policies implemented by the various levels of government and apply intact regardless of the extent of vertical redistribution pursued by governments. They can be looked at as policies that facilitate the decentralization of fiscal responsibilities, ensuring that the benefits of decentralization are achieved without compromising national objectives of efficiency and equity.

It appears as if there is a clear vertical imbalance in India between (1) the powers of taxation assigned to the Union and the states and (2) the social and economic responsibilities assigned to the states. That is, the states' responsibilities exceed their own-source revenues. This arrangement is intended to permit each order of government to do what it is thought to do best; that is, it recognizes that the Centre is perhaps in the best position to collect certain kinds of taxes and to expend and redistribute tax revenues for equitable purposes nationwide, while states and their local governments are in the best position to manage developmental programs and to deliver most services because they are closest to the people.

From federal point of view,'State' is an exercise into creation of 'unit of self rule' through which autonomy of the society (in terms of maintenance of identity and assured development) gets operationalized. People having distinct socio-cultural identity, concentrated in few contiguous districts within the existing state-systems, seek a separate state in order to preserve, protect and promote their identity. Like in Telengana, it is argued that a separate state would provide them a political identity and a constitutionally documented institutional space for interest articulation and protection within the broader territorial state In India, the unit of ‚self rule' may be :(i) a full-fledged state; (ii) autonomous region or regional councils with adequate legislative and executive powers within the existing states in which they are included; (iii) district development council with adequate authority over local planning for the people located in 'ethnic enclaves' of an otherwise composite state; and (iv) granting of Union Territory status to city regions, strategically important region or sub-region and to those areas which are extremely backward. Statehood may be granted to those regional communities which do qualify the three-point criteria of:

(i) administrative and political manageability involving closer contact between the people and their elected representatives;
(ii) techno-economic viability; and
(iii) socio-cultural homogeneity (in terms of tribes\ jatis, language\ dialect, belief system\ religious communities and ethnic identities)".

In order to promote federal stability at the macro level, the institutions of shared rule such as Zonal Councils, Inter-state Councils, etc., need to be activised. These institutions are advisory or recommendatory bodies, facilitating inter-state cooperation and coordination in the areas of national and regional planning and development.

During the first half a century of India's independence, there were two opposing views regarding the formation and reorganization of states. One, held by the Union was that states should be economically viable and administratively convenient. The other, held by emerging groups, was that where there was a sense of community, or consciousness of a separate identity, then, if feasible, that community should form a separate state. Arguments in favor of the formation or reorganization of states, among others, have been geographical proximity, a common language, similar usages and customs, comparable socio-economic and political stages of development, common historical traditions and experiences, a common way of living, administrative expediency, and, more than anything else, a widely prevalent sentiment of „togetherness", that is, a sense of identity.

The two views clashed but, over time, the second view prevailed. Then, the States' Reorganization Commission 1955 (SRC) laid down four principles for determining and demarcating the boundary of a state. They were;

(i) preservation and strengthening of the unity and security of India
(ii) linguistic and cultural homogeneity,
(iii) financial, economic and administrative considerations; and
(iv) successful working of a national plan.

The re-organization was also not complete because all the linguistic areas were not given a territorial recognition. These regions were often not treated as politically coherent units reflecting the aspirations of their inhabitants to manage their own affairs. In this competition for resources, the regions used several benchmarks to establish their identity. They were language, culture, economic advancement, administrative coherence, and even the socio-economic backwardness of the region (due to its being part of a bigger regional unit). Regional movements sparked demands for the formation of new states, and for the reorganization of existing states. These demands did not usually go beyond claiming resource-sharing within the broader national context. In this, language was often the symbol giving expression to these aspirations. Generally speaking, the national leadership never anticipated the evolution of social, economic and historical imbalances between historically defined regions in a state.

Parts of India are inhabited by "tribals" and so-called "hill people" who often are not part of the "mainstream". They may live in particular regions of specific states. Such regions have demanded a separate state if they have felt discriminated against and deprived of development, and also if they feel that through resource-transfers others are prospering at their expense. This is what happened to regions such as Marathawada, Vidarbha, and Konkam (in Maharashtra), Jharkhand (in Bihar), and Chhattisgarh (in Madhya Pradesh). The demands for statehood by tribal people in Jharkand, and by hill people in Uttaranchal, were based on the perception that they were victims of an internal colonialism by other regional and cultural groups. Then, there are other parts of India that are quite prosperous. Here a relatively rich region (in terms of resources or agricultural and industrial output) may resent having to support one that is backward. An example of such a region is one in the more developed western part of the state of Uttar Pradesh, one that calls itself "Harit Pradesh."

A close scrutiny of state-formation in India would reveal that, together with languages, many variable and critical factors like ethnic-cum-economic consideration (Nagaland, Meghalaya, Manipur and Tripura); religion, script and sentiments (Haryana and Punjab); language-cum-culture (Maharashtra and Gujarat); historical and political factors (Uttar Pradesh and Bihar); integration of Princely states and the need for viable groupings (Madhya Pradesh and Rajasthan) and of course, language-cum-social distinctiveness (Tamilnadu, Kerala, Mysore, Andhra Pradesh, Assam, Bengal and Orissa) have played a decisive role in the composition of the Indian federation.

It is a fact that most of the demands for constituting new states have been primarily based on allegedly unfair and unequal distribution of development benefits and expenditures in multi-lingual states. If people have to live in the territory of the others, they may feel dominated. The success of their demands is related to the success of the elite in marketing the perception of deprivation and in making an "imagined community" into a natural one. Because numbers count, in a democratic process, the forging of several identities into a common identity is politically expedient.

When the people are made partners in governance, the nation as such is strengthened. Comparable development is possible elsewhere with the decentralization of power, and may lessen the demands for separate states. One should not rush to assume that granting more administrative and fiscal powers to the states, or creating a large number of states, may weaken the country.

The system can work if we accept that power belongs to the people who give it to the next tier upward, and then next tier further upward. In the so-called empowerment of the local-level governments, actually the power gets transferred from one set of elite to another. In the Indian rural power-structure, so much of inequality exists that this empowerment may actually strengthen inequality and oppression.

Cooperative federalism can succeed only if a fair balance is maintained between the claims of diversity and the requirements of unity. If that is absent, whatever mechanisms of inter-governmental relations are devised would remain non-functional and ineffective. The constitutional provisions stipulate that the state shall decide about the resource-transfers to local bodies. The principle of governance is that the government should meet its expenditure or, at least, revenue on core services should come from its own resources. This should be by right and not through benevolence of any other government. What needs to be transferred is a power to collect resources, to garner resources, and the power to tax. Unless that is there, local units remain locally dependent units, not local self-governing units.

Decentralised and grass-root planning and implementation are features of shared governance; and this, in turn, reflects the correct image of federal governance. Social federalism cannot be sidelined in the name of political federalism.

The National Commission to Review the Working of the Constitution had observed that:

"The subjects given under the Sixth Schedule and those mentioned in the Eleventh Schedule could be entrusted to the Autonomous District Councils (ADCs). The system of in-built safeguards in the Sixth Schedule should be maintained and strengthened for the minority and micro-minority groups while empowering them with greater responsibilities and opportunities, for example, through the process of Central funding for Plan expenditure instead of routing all funds through the state Governments. The North-Eastern Council can play a central role here by developing a process of public education on the proposed changes, which would assure communities about protection of their traditions and also bring in gender representation and give voice to other ethnic groups."

There are both formal institutional and informal political arrangements for Centre-state coordination. Among the formal mechanisms are the Planning Commission, Finance Commission, National Development Council, Inter-state Council, National Integration Council, zonal councils, tribunals for adjudicating specific disputes, and various commissions and committees to look into specific aspects of Union-state relations.. The informal mechanisms include ministerial and departmental meetings, conferences of constitutional functionaries and of political executives, and the governors' and chief ministers' conferences that are convened by the president and the prime minister. These informal arrangements are aimed at laying down procedural norms of conduct, particularly over such issues as the sharing of central taxes and the Union's intervention in states' affairs, and at evolving a common policy on such trans-governmental issues as the environment, communications, and health. Similarly, such informal mechanisms evolve conventions of governance on questions of states' rights, interstate trade and commerce, sharing of river waters, interstate communications, and other matters.

Notes

1. Akhtar Majeed, Ronald R. Watts, Douglas M. Brown, *Distribution of Powers and Responsibilities in Federal Polities*, (Montreal: McGill Queens, 2006).
2. Albert Breton, "Supplementary Statement," Royal Commission on the Economic Union and Development Prospects for Canada, *Report*, Vol. 3, (Ottawa: Supply and Services Canada, 1985), pp. 486-526.
3. M.Guibernau and J. Hutchinson, *Understanding Nationalism, Cambridge 2001*, J. Hutchinson, *Modern Nationalism,* London 1994, M. Moore, *The Ethics of Nationalism*, (OUP, 2001), G. Smith, *Federalism: The Multi-Ethnic Challenge*, (London, 1995).
4. Granvile Austin, *Working a Democratic Constitution*, (New Delhi: Oxford, 1999), pp. 560-4.
5. Supreme Court of India in *S.R. Bommai v Union of India*, 3 SCC (1994) quoted in A.G. Noorani, *Constitutional Questions in India*, (New Delhi: Oxford, 2000), p. 268.

11

Public Policy and Social Accountability for Federal Governance

No principle of fiscal federalism was actually violated when the Prime Minister of India, some time back, asked the state governments to ponder for themselves whether the Union's funds for rural development were being properly used by the states. It is hardly a secret that out of these Rs 17,000 crores, annually made available by the Union, only a fraction manages to reach the intended beneficiaries. Any sound fiscal system would involve some monitoring by the fund-giving authority.

Accountability Vs Competence

The political controversy over this issue missed one point: if any monitoring by the Union over the states—as far as funding of local bodies is concerned—is an attempt to further centralisation, so is the financial choking of the local bodies by the state governments. It is not as if federalism is in jeopardy when the Union does something that the states do not like, but federalism is safe when the states do not provide competence to the local bodies. The point that is missed is that the Union and the states are not the only constituents of our federalism; there is a third-tier also at the local level.

The debate focuses on the constitutional division of responsibilities between the Union and the states and this, supposedly, is the basis of India's federal structure. Responsibilities of various tiers of government are determined by the functions that are assigned to them. The ability and competence to perform these functions depend on the earmarking of sources of finance. Any efficient demarcation of functions and finances is possible if a cost-effective analysis is first made of the efficiency of different tiers to undertake some functions. This has to be followed by some monitoring to assess how successfully, effectively and efficiently the resources were utilised by a government. 'Process Improvement' in industrial management involves removing a few layers, and this results in speedy and effective disbursement. If Panchayati Raj Institutions (PRIs) are to be made effective in self-governance then they have to benefit those for whom they were meant and created. Their total dependence on the state government funding, and the reluctance of the latter to share power, does not allow the PRIs to make their presence felt.

By constitutional amendments, rural and urban local bodies have also been provided with specific domains of governance. The starting point has to be not just distribution of functions but transferring functions to these bodies and allocating funds to them, thus making them competent to perform the functions constitutionally assigned to them.

If the Panchayat bodies are to seen only as mechanisms of carrying out certain programmes then perhaps the present system may work because they tend to function only as executive extension of implementation. They have become like government agencies. But if we want Panchayats and urban local bodies to function as real units of local self-government, then they should also have separate competence, functions and resources. Also, they need to function more closely with community-based organisations, with the user-groups or stakeholders in development. Presently, the question of management of rural resources is inter-woven within the framework of induced governance. Any rural governance is effectively possible only if it has an access to rural resources because governance presupposes efficient management of resources.

Necessary provisions need to be made so that 'gram sabhas' are vested with approving and sanctioning powers as well as monitoring the functions. If they are made a parliament at the grassroot level then no work would be taken at that level by the government agencies without the approval and consent of a gram sabhas. But the question is: Are we ready to share the power?

Instead of looking at Good Governance, or framework of institutions merely as an efficient management of resources, the emphasis needs to be on the questions of access to resources. The stake-holder approach of governance would require first making the user-group competent before expecting it to effectively manage the resources.

Just a legislation is not enough to bring about some transformation unless it is separately translated into practice. Even after a decade, Panchayats have yet to emerge as institutions of self-governance. There are Questions of mandatory and enabling provisions and what is missing is empowerment. Unless the implementation of constitutional provisions regarding Panchayats is made mandatory, there would be room for manipulation by the states. States have in effect made Panchayats their agencies and this would continue until clear-cut allocation of powers and functions is made for Panchayats and municipalities in the 11th and 12th schedule of a Constitution.

The sub-state (3rd tier) level of Indian federal polity is comprised of 532 District panchayats, 5912 Block panchayats and 2 31 630 Village panchayats which, taken together, elect 3 million representatives every five years. For making the Panchayats fiscally self-sufficient, the Constitution 73rd Amendment (in 1992) incorporated additional clauses Art. 243 H and I, through which a state Legislature may (a) authorise a panchayat to levy, collect and appropriate such taxes, duties, tolls and fees in accordance with such procedure and subject to such limits; (b) assign to a panchayat such taxes...fees and collected by the state government for such purposes and subjects to such conditions and limits; (c) provide for making such grants in aid to the panchayats from the consolidated fund of the state; and (d) provide for constitution of such funds for crediting all money received respectively, by or on behalf of the panchayats and also for the withdrawl of such money therefore. A provision was thus made for the constitution of a state Finance Commission in each state for reviewing the financial position of the panchayat. bodies and determining the principles for sharing funds (both tax and grants in aid) between the state and the panchayat bodies. However, the Constitutional amendments pertaining to Panchayats and urban local governments are rather vague about their expenditure functions and revenue sources. The actual assignment is to be done by the state legislatures, on the recommendations of the state Finance Commissions, appointed by the state. But the state government is under no obligation to accept these recommendations. The indifference of some states to Panchayats and urban local governments is obvious from the fact that they have not appointed state Finance Commissions, and in some states these Commissions have not made their recommendations, and a few others have yet to accept the recommendations made by their Commissions. In many cases, the state Commissions have curtailed the access of the Panchayats to buoyant taxes. Major sources of revenue, like Sales tax and Excise duty, are not shared with the Panchayats which can just levy license fee on trade and profession.

Urban and local governments (Municipalities and Panchayats) receive grants from their state governments for discharging responsibilities under their jurisdiction. Since their power and scope of raising resources on their own is narrow and limited, grants given to them are crucial for discharging any function. Yet, the states clamour for more fiscal powers and a larger share of Union's resources but are not willing to share their resources with the local bodies. The state governments give to the local bodies both the grants-in-aid and grants-in-incentive. The latter are matching grants and the local bodies are expected to mobilise/ raise higher resources to become eligible for state incentives. The preference of the local bodies is, understandably, for untied grants-in-aid instead of project-tied grants. It appears as if grants play a negative role in inducing the recipient to raise own resources. Such an assertion can be, to some extent, true in the relationship between the Union and the states. But the local bodies have such a limited scope for revenue generation, and relatively a vast area of jurisdiction, that they are perenially dependent upon the states for the latter's grants. Some of the direct taxes that used to bring the bulk of revenue sources for the urban local bodies included property tax, entertainment tax and motor-vehicle tax. While the last two are now with the state governments, restrictions have have been placed on the property tax and its returns are very low. The best indirect tax for these bodies, Octroi, that used to provide maximum yield has been abolished. There are certain insignificant incomes such as surcharge on Stamp Duty and cess on land revenue etc that are shared between the state governments and the local bodies. Consequently, the local bodies have to depend almost entirely on state governments for discharging responsibilities assigned to them. Now that the former have been entrusted with far more responsibilities, it appears appropriate that high-yielding sales tax and state excise duty are brought under the divisible category. The constitutional difficulty is in the fact that devolution of powers and responsibilities for Panchayats are listed but an elaborate scheme has not been provided regarding their sources of finance. Thus, what has been decentralised is the assignment of functions and not the resources. Further, because the state governments are reluctant to part with revenue-generating powers, fiscal autonomy is actually denied to the Panchayats.

The Presidential Proclamation (3 June 1998) establishing the Eleventh Finance Commission had asked it to recommend measures for augmenting the resources of the Panchayats on the basis of the recommendations of the State Finance Commissions. The consolidated funds of the states were to be augmented so as to supplement the resources of the Panchayats. Accordingly, to make the Panchayats financially viable, the Commission recommended: (a) to allow the state to adopt three or two tiers systems of Panchayati Raj with greater efficiency and economy, (b) to levy taxes on land-based taxes, and profession tax either by the state or local bodies, (c) to periodically review the rate-structure of the user charges levied by the Panchayats, (d) to build database on the finances of the Panchayats, (e) to transfer functions and powers to Panchayats in accordance with Art 343 G and 11th Schedule, (f) to constitute district planning committees (g) to provide an annual grant of Rs 1600 crores for the Panchayats. The Commission evolved an index of decentralisation based on some parameters for determining funds-allocation to the Panchayats: enactment of state Panchayat legislation, intervention in the functioning of the Panchayats, assignment of functions, transfer of functions to Panchayats by way of rules, assignment of taxation powers, levy of taxes by Panchayats, constitution of the state Finance Commissions, and submission of action-taken reports, action taken on the recommendations of the State Finance Commissions, election to Panchayats, and constitution of District Planning Committees. The Commission's recommendations were intended to make Panchayats competent with powers and authority so that they may discharge their responsibilities as institutions of self-government: preparing plans for social justice and economic development, and implementing schemes towards this end entrusted to them, including the ones listed in the Constitution's 11th Schedule: agriculture, minor irrigation, small industries, rural roads, rural electrification, education, health and sanitation, public distribution system, maintenance of community assets, poverty alleviation etc.

It is not uncommon, for some of the states, to delay the transfer of funds received from the Union for the PRIs. The actual assignment of expenditure functions and revenue sources is done by the state legislatures, on the recommendations of the state Finance Commissions, appointed by the state. But the state government is under no obligation to accept these recommendations. The indifference of some states to Panchayats and urban local governments is obvious from the fact that they have not appointed state Finance Commissions, and in some states these Commissions have not made their recommendations, and a few others have yet to accept the recommendations made by their Commissions.

In many of the spheres of state activity, the Union government has already stepped in, not through any constitutional provision, but through the process of administration. No allegations have come to notice of dismantling of the federal polity. In matters of implementation of plan policies in areas of land-reforms, forest development, development of rural industries, irrigation, cooperative farming, agriculture, education, health, cottage industries etc, the Planning Commission insists on uniform policies to be followed by the states. Most of these areas are the ones that come under the ambit of rural-development or under the nominal jurisdictions of the PRIs. It is believed that though the primary responsibility in such matters is of state governments, the Union has an overall responsibility for helping coordinate and guide the work of the states so that national policies can be satisfactorily worked out.

Centralised decision-making in resource-allocation continues to erode the federal spirit but it is not questioned when the issues pertain to the Union-state relations. It appears that there is a lurking suspicion at the Union level that the state governments do not give adequate priority to some nationally important activities, particularly in the fields of social policies. Much of the centralisation has been the result of a belief that Union investments in states benefit more states, particularly in areas and in amounts that the states either could not afford or were unwilling to step into, like the areas earmarked for the local bodies. With the rolling back of the government through various dis-investments, no doubt it would not be an active entity in production and distribution activities. But there is nothing to preclude its regulation and control. Till the market-regulation is decentralised, at the social level, the state and local-level governments would continue to hopelessly depend on the Union. Both the Union and the states can legislate on economic and social planning, and there are a number of subjects in the States' list which are relevant to planning. Since the Union law prevails in the event of jurisdiction dispute between the Union and the states, the Union can go to any extent in the name of planning. Though this should have been treated as a violation of the federal spirit, the states do not complain because ultimately they get to benefit.

In India, the inter-governmental fiscal agencies have not acquired the functional relevance visualized in the Constitution. Their recommendations have lacked any force and they have not been in a position to cope with the inter-jurisdictional strains of the Indian fiscal federal set-up. This is due to the ad hoc style of their functioning and this has eroded their credibility. Cooperative federalism can succeed only if a fair balance is maintained between the claims of diversity and the requirements of unity. If that is absent, whatever mechanisms of inter-governmental relations are devised would remain non-functional and ineffective. The constitutional provisions stipulate that the state shall decide about the resource-transfers to local bodies. Any transfer mechanism increases the dependence of the local level units.

Populist enthusiasm for laying foundation-stones for projects that are not eventually completed does not benefit the acclaimed beneficiaries. Decentralised and grass-root planning and implementation are features of shared governance; and this, in turn, reflects the correct image of federal governance. Social federalism cannot be sidelined in the name of political federalism. If the governance is to be people-centred then it has to conform to public accountability.

The Government says that "We want to make India a developed nation." We know that to realise this vision, the only way is through a partnership between the Government and the people, between the Government and business, and between the Government and non-governmental organizations." "Is this a dream? Yes. Is this an impossible dream? 'No.' So, the thinking of the Government is that what we are going to achieve may be a dream but it is not an impossible dream. So, what exactly is that dream and how has it come about?

It was not the Constitution which had failed the Indian state or the Indian nation. It was not the Indian state that failed the country. It may be various Governments. We could not be up to that task of achieving what we were enjoying and what we were expected to do because the Constitution of India had created a balance - a balance as far as the governance part is concerned, a creative balance between an effective Centre and effectively empowered states. In spite of various problems of balance maintenance, the system has survived though many of its federal features got eroded in that process.

This socio-economic, political and different types of diversity of the country had made cooperative aspects of federalism much more important. Whereas cooperative federalism can be based on some commonality of interests, the bargaining aspects depend on the consensual interest of constituent units. Though the cooperative federalism can be the desire, the bargaining aspects of federalism are the reality in Indian polity.

Now it has been assumed over the years that a good governance is possible only if the Government is stable. But no stability is possible without the empowerment of all the sections of our society. What is actually termed as instability, in fact, is a manifestation of the electorate's dissatisfaction with the performance of the power elite. And it is erroneous to believe that political instability would result if the Government is not stable or durable. We should not confuse regime instability or the governmental instability with the political instability or the constitutional instability. There is a lot of difference between that. We have witnessed profound political instability when the Central Government was supposedly very strong. We have witnessed political stability when the Central Government has been comprised of desperate political parties fighting for their survival, fighting for their mutual interests and intermingling of various interests.

Another issue for consideration is the problem of law and order. These are the issues, as from the law and order point of view, which do not concern only one state and where the specific authority of the state concerned can no longer be applicable. There are various crimes which are borderless in nature and may happen in one state but they would affect the life of persons in other states also. They are transnational crimes like international terrorism. Similarly, there are trans-state crimes like black-marketing anything, money laundering, drugs and similar issues, including terrorism, within the country. All of them can be brought together in war by proxy means. They are a war on the state. They are a war on the country. Even a normal crime, which affects more than one state, is a crime for more than a state. Just taking this plea that law and order is a state subject and, therefore, federal government cannot interfere in that, is not going to remain valid for a long period. Creating a system of federal forces is an entirely different thing. But we cannot overlook this issue that, sooner or later, we have to take up this question seriously that there are crimes which affect more than one state and the plea would not be sufficient enough that law and order is a state subject. So, on that basis, if we have to have governance, we must have a balance as far as decentralization and more powers for the Union Government are concerned. That balance was provided by the Constitution of India and that balance is still valid.

Further Readings

Burges, Michael and Alain-G, Gagnon, (eds.), *Comparative Federalism and Federation: Competing Trends and Future Directions,* (Hemel Hempstead: Harvester Wheatsheaf, 1993).

De Villiers, Bertus, (ed.), *Evaluating federal Systems,* (Cape Town: Jutta & Co., 1994).

Elaigwu, J. Isawa, *Foundations of Nigerian Federalism 1960-1995* (Abuja: NCIR, 1996).

Elazar, Daniel J., (ed.), *Federal Systems of the World: A Handbook of Federal,* Confederal and Autonomy Arrangements, 2nd (ed.), (Harlow: Longman Group Limited, 1994).

Franks, C.E.S., *Parliament, Intergovernmental Relations, and National Unity,* (Kingston, Queen's University: Institute for Intergovernmental Relations, 1999[a]).

Galligan, Brian, *A Federal Republic: Australia's Constitutional System of Government,* (Oakleigh, Melbourne: Cambridge University Press, 1995).

Jeffery, C., (ed.), *Recasting German Federalism,* (London and New York: Pinter, 1999).

Majeed, Akhtar, *Federalism Within the Union,* (New Delhi: Manak, 2004).

Simeon, Richard (ed.), *Intergovernmental Relations,* (Toronto: University of Toronto Press, 1985).

Verney, Douglas V., "Federalism, Federative Systems, and Federations: The United States, Canada and India," *Publius: The Journal of Federalism,* 25:2 (1995): 81-97.

Watts, R.L., *Comparing Federal Systems,* (Montreal and Kingston: McGill-Queen's University Press, 1966).

Index